his
brother's
keeper

his
brother's
keeper

Charles M.
Sheldon

Updated by Jim Reimann

Publishers Since 1798

THOMAS NELSON PUBLISHERS®
Nashville

Published in Nashville, Tennessee, by Thomas Nelson, Inc.

The Bible version used in this publication is THE NEW KING JAMES VERSION.
Copyright © 1979, 1980, 1982, Thomas Nelson, Inc., Publishers.

ISBN 0-7852-6948-7

Printed in the United States of America.

1 2 3 4 5 6 BVG 04 03 02 01 00 99

contents

foreword

The original edition of *His Brother's Keeper* was written by Charles M. Sheldon in 1895, one year before he wrote *In His Steps,* the multimillion-copy best-seller. Of course, *In His Steps* is the story that launched the recent "WWJD" phenomenon, which asks the question, "What would Jesus do?"

His Brother's Keeper, although similar in style to *In His Steps,* is based upon real events. In it you will find a fascinating account of a true-life labor struggle, not unlike many fought today. It is interesting sometimes when looking back, even more than a hundred years, to realize that the more things seem to change, the more human issues stay the same. You will also find the story of a spiritual struggle raging within the soul of the main character, Stuart Duncan.

As Stuart's story unfolds, he must come to terms with the fact that there must be more to life than money. He is a wealthy young man who learns quite quickly that money will not buy happiness or fulfillment, or even a settlement in a labor dispute before it becomes violent.

The story revolves around the concept of stewardship. The characters face the challenge of how, in practical ways, they can invest not only their money, but also their time, their talents, and their very lives to make a difference in this world.

It is an adventure story, a drama, a love story, a management-versus-labor story, a rich-versus-poor story, and a spiritual journey all rolled into one enjoyable book. Sheldon used this book to instruct his church members. In fact, you can see in his preface that he read this book chapter by chapter to his congregation on Sunday evenings. When I first read that, my thought was, *That was a bit presumptuous of him—reading his book to his church members.* But later, as I thought more about it, I remembered that Jesus used parables, or storytelling, in exactly the same way and for the same reason—to teach godly principles and truths.

The fact that Sheldon read this to his entire congregation meant that he believed its message was important and understandable for all ages. As I have worked on updating the language of this new edition, I have endeavored to keep you, the reader, in mind. The events of the story remain unchanged, but the language is that of today. My work on the updated editions of *My Utmost for His Highest* and *Streams in the Desert* taught me how quickly language changes over the years, and the 104-year-old language of *His Brother's Keeper* was no exception.

It is an honor for me to be bringing this recently rediscovered book to a new generation of readers. *His Brother's Keeper* has apparently been "lost" for more than half of the years since its original publication. My prayer is that you will not only enjoy reading it, but that God would use it to guide you in His ways. I see it as a wonderful story for those who know Him and want to know Him better, and others who are simply seeking the way of truth, but have not yet found it.

Enjoy!

—Jim Reimann, 1999

preface

His Brother's Keeper was written during the winter of 1895 and first read, one chapter at a time, on successive Sunday evenings to my congregation in the Central Church.

The scenes in the mining region are based upon events which occurred during the great strike among the iron miners in the summer of 1895, and which were witnessed by the author.

The Salvation Army songs are exact copies of songs actually sung by the Army.

—Charles M. Sheldon

1

the
big
strike

I just heard that five thousand miners have gone out on strike at the Champion and DeMott mines this morning," said one of the train passengers to the young man seated next to him as they slowly pulled into the station.

"I wonder if that's true," his friend replied.

"Well, *something* strange is happening. Got to run—this is my stop! I'm sure we'll hear all about it soon enough." He then grabbed his bag and hurriedly stepped onto the railway platform.

The station was entirely deserted, except for a few railroad employees. The young man looked around a moment as if he were expecting someone, and then walked quickly across the platform and around the corner of the station. From that side of the building the town and its public square were in full view. Suddenly, his curiosity was piqued because what he saw was quite unusual for his little town.

The public square was a small park with a stage platform in the middle, and it was located at the convergence of seven streets. Each of the streets seemed to wander down the hills from the different mining districts. They started as mere footpaths used by the miners, but then developed into small lanes of country roads, lined by fragments of wooden sidewalks as they approached the town. Finally, they grew into paved streets with cement sidewalks, and with stores and office buildings on both sides. Facing the park, and directly in front of the stage, stood a large church, which with its property covered the entire block. The railway station formed one side of the heptagon made by the convergence of these streets, while another church, two streets down from the other, formed yet another side. The rest of the buildings bordering the park were stores, offices of various mining companies, and a large hotel.

It was here in the heart of this little mining town of Champion, on this very morning in 1895, that Stuart Duncan saw the largest crowd of people he had ever seen gathered in town. Stuart was the son of Ross Duncan, owner of the largest mines in Champion. He was thirty years old, had finished his college education, and was just now returning home from a year of traveling in Europe. He stepped down from the railway station platform and pushed his way into the crowd. As he did, he thought to himself that in all his travels abroad he had not seen anything to compare with this unusual gathering in this mining town where he had been raised prior to going to college in the East.

The moment he stepped into the crowd several voices called out, "Stuart, give us your help!" The voices carried differing accents, from Cornish, to Finnish, to English, to Irish, and to Scottish. He noticed the subdued action of the men—they were excited, but under control. The stage was crowded with familiar faces, but Stuart Duncan looked directly at only one. It was the face of a short but muscular young man. He had removed his hat and was standing on the bench at the edge of the stage. He had thick black hair, deeply set black eyes, thick eyebrows, other strong facial features, yet a smooth face, and a short, round neck. He was leaning forward a little, had his left hand wrapped around one of the roof supports of the stage, and gently waved his old hat up and down with his right hand.

Stuart moved closer to the stage until he was within speaking distance. As he wedged himself closer, he was finally stopped by the great sea of humanity. Several people greeted him, yet quietly, for the crowd seemed focused on the young man who stood leaning over them.

"What's happening here? What's the problem?" Stuart asked the men around him. "What's Eric doing up there?"

Before anyone could answer, the young man standing on the bench began to speak. His words came very slowly, as if every one of them was being thought out carefully. He stopped moving and stood perfectly still. The large crowd in the square was so quiet that it reminded Stuart of a special service he had once attended in an English cathedral. Four thousand people had knelt in total silence before the service began.

"Brothers," said Eric, "this is no ordinary event in the history of labor. What we have done, and are about to do, carries serious consequences. We have made demands for sufficient wages to comfortably sustain us and our families during this coming winter. It has been refused, so we have walked out of the mines determined to defend our rights—strongly, yet peacefully." Eric paused a moment, and Stuart noticed how his grip on the roof post appeared to tighten. As he continued, the crowd seemed even more quiet.

"Brothers, we need more than human wisdom at a time like this. It is fitting that we bow our heads and seek divine help."

Every head was uncovered as each person removed his hat for prayer. Then the speaker's voice rang out clearly and strongly above the crowd.

"Lord, we need Your help today. We ask for wisdom and to know

Your will. O Lord, keep us from lawlessness in our protest! Keep us all from drunkenness, violence, and injury to anyone's life or property. We ask simply for our rights as men, and for sufficient wages to live in basic comfort. Show us what to do, and keep us from evil. Lord, bless these men who work with their hands, and bless our families. We ask this in Jesus' name. Amen."[1]

As Eric finished his prayer, he raised his head, and the miners then put on their hats. Stuart peered out over the heads of the crowd and up to Eric. His eyes then looked beyond the town to the pine-covered hills dotted with mining engine houses and stockpiles of ore. He noticed the smoke curling from the furnace smokestacks and said to himself, "The pumps must still be running." The whole scene was very vivid to him. The crowd, the churches, the park, the stage, the hills, the mines, and that familiar face of his friend above him—every detail of this human drama seemed to pierce his heart. But the greatest shock to his nerves was that brief prayer. It seemed so strange and unusual—much like a story—not real life.

Suddenly, Eric was speaking again. He appealed to the miners to watch their conduct because the world would be watching them. He spoke just as he had prayed—slowly and carefully. As he finished, he caught sight of Stuart.

Eric's face flushed for a moment as the eyes of the two men met. The look on each of their faces seemed to say, "I wonder if he is still the same?"

The clock in the steeple of the larger of the two churches struck eight. Eric jumped down from the bench, and another miner took his place and spoke in an even more impassioned tone to the men. The men cheered and waved their hats in the air. Stuart gradually worked his way through the crowd, while being frequently stopped by acquaintances. When he stood before the church with the clock tower, he eagerly looked for someone from his own home. Suddenly, the strong voice of a man standing on the church steps above him boomed, "Stuart! When did you join the strike?"

"Doctor!" cried Stuart eagerly with a smile of welcome that wonderfully lit up his thoughtful face. "Except for my father or Louise, you are the very person I most wanted to see. In fact, where are they? They were supposed to meet me at the train station this morning. Isn't this strike an astounding event? Please tell me all about it."

The doctor shrugged his shoulders. "You know as much about it as I do. The men walked out this morning without notice. The Freeport, Vasplaine, and DeMott miners are all here with the Champion men. They walked over from the lower range early this morning."

"What do the men want?" Stuart asked vaguely. He had so many questions, but this was the first he blurted out.

The doctor shrugged his shoulders again. "The contract miners want two dollars a day, the tram operators one seventy-five, and the men at the top one fifty."

"Who is the leader of the men?"

"You just saw him! Eric Vassall. And it seems like only yesterday you two men were young kids in short pants running through the mines and worrying the miners to death with your silly pranks. And now Eric is the leader of the biggest mining strike in history, playing the role of prophet, priest, and who knows what all. And you—"

"And I," interrupted Stuart with another smile as he pulled the doctor down from the step above him, "I am—at least so far—nobody, until I've eaten my breakfast. I can't understand where my father and Louise can be. Have you seen them this morning?"

"No. Get into my buggy. I'll take you up to the house."

The doctor's office faced the square, and his horse and buggy stood nearby. Stuart glanced back at the crowd as he and the doctor started up the street.

"It is a remarkable scene. I did not witness anything quite like it abroad. I saw several strikes in England, Germany, and France while I was away, but I've never known one to be opened with prayer. Have you, Doctor?"

"No," replied the doctor dryly.

Stuart looked at him. He was driving, as he always did, with one foot outside the buggy. He loosely and carelessly held the reins in one hand, while the horse madly raced up the sandy red iron-ore street. They had quickly left the paved road and were headed up a steep lane cut through one of the many hills surrounding the town. Yes, the doctor always drove that way, and Stuart used to say that riding with him was as exciting as working in a gunpowder mill during a thunderstorm.

"I get the sense you don't believe Eric's prayer was sincere," Stuart surmised from the doctor's facial expression.

"Sincere enough. But what's the use? We all know how the strike will end—prayer or no prayer."

"What's happened to Eric, Doctor? He never used to be religious. At least not like this."

"Salvation Army," replied the doctor briefly.

"Oh!" Stuart was still puzzled. He would have to talk it over with Eric. There was so much to talk about since he had left a year ago. So many critical issues had arisen in their lives that needed to be discussed. But as they rode along, he was growing anxious about his father and sister. It seemed very strange that they had not met him at the station. Perhaps the strike had kept his father busy. In any case, his homecoming had so far been much different from what he had anticipated.

The family house sat back from the road on the side of the hill. It was a beautiful brick mansion, surrounded by a dozen huge pines. Stuart loved the place because so many special memories had been made there. He had no memory whatsoever of any other house, although he had been born in one of the eastern states. It was in this house that his mother had died when he was ten years old. He owed his thoughtful, romantic, and truthful nature to her. On the other hand, he had inherited his slow stubbornness and occasional outbursts of passionate feelings from his father. He thought of all the happy times in the old house where as a boy, and later as a college student, he had enjoyed all the luxuries of wealth, leisure, and friendship.

Suddenly, a man pulled out of the road into which he and the doctor were just now turning to head up to the house. Both men pulled up on the reins just in time to avoid running into each other.

"Is that you, Dr. Saxon?" shouted the man. "I was just heading to see you. Mr. Duncan has been hurt. The horses ran away this morning, and—"

Stuart did not wait to hear more. He jumped out of the buggy and at a full run cut across the grounds in front of the house. The doctor shouted at his horse, and with one short stroke of the whip the buggy dashed up the driveway like a whirlwind. At the end of the long veranda he stopped just long enough to jump out, while letting the horse go on to the barn. He was so quick that as he reached the large front door he met Stuart bounding up the veranda steps.

"Now then, my boy," said the doctor quietly, filling up the doorway with his large frame and getting directly in front of Stuart. "Don't get excited. This is my case, not yours."

"Let me by!" cried Stuart, his face flooded with passion. "He's my father! And he may be dying! What right do you have to stand in my way?"

"Very well." The doctor spoke softly, almost like a child. He stepped aside and began to walk slowly down the porch steps. "You have inherited the Duncan passion for perfection, but if your father dies through your nonsensical exercise of it, don't blame me."

Stuart took one step and grabbed the doctor's arm. "Come back!" he said. All his passion subsided in an instant. "I will behave like you. Please come! Perhaps you will need my help."

The doctor stared intently at Stuart, and then quickly turned around and entered the house with him. This incident would mean nothing without understanding what was at stake because of it. Dr. Saxon had good reason to believe that the life of the son in this case was endangered by the great fits of emotional excitement that would occasionally rage through him like a storm. An attempt to comfort his father under these conditions might have serious consequences to them both.

The servants inside the house were running around in a state of total confusion. The doctor stopped one of them and said sternly, "Are you all crazy here? Where is Mr. Duncan?"

"They carried him into the north room," was the answer.

"North room! You might as well have carried him to the North Pole and left him to die! Quickly, Stuart, send one of the men to my office for my black bag, and then hurry back to your father."

The doctor went down the long hall, turned right into another hallway, and entered a large room at the end. Lying across the bed in the middle of the room was a young woman. Her arms were folded over the face of the man who lay there, and she had fainted in that position. The doctor lifted her up just as Stuart reentered the room.

"O God! Not Louise too!" he cried.

The doctor gave him a calming look and replied, "No, she has simply fainted. Now then, stay calm and help me here. Look after your sister while I see to your father."

He placed Louise in Stuart's arms who, with the servant's help, quickly brought her back to consciousness. Meanwhile, the doctor turned to the man on the bed and masterfully proceeded to do all that his skill, training, and years of practice could do.

Ross Duncan lay on the bed like a dead man. His build was muscular, and he appeared very stern and harsh, even though he helplessly lay there. There was a terrible gash over one of his eyes. He was covered with blood and dust, bruised from head to toe, and his clothes were torn and disheveled. Yet he had not lost consciousness, and with the iron will that so characterized him, he managed to let the doctor know his wishes.

"All right, all right, Mr. Duncan," said the doctor in reply to a whisper from the wounded man. "I won't give you any anesthetic if you don't want it. But I do have to sew up this little cut above your eye. Has that slow turtle gotten back with my case yet?" he asked Stuart, who had left Louise a minute to come over to the bed.

"He hasn't had time yet, Doctor."

"Why didn't he take my horse?" growled the doctor. "How is Louise?"

"Better. What a terrible fall Father must have had!"

Stuart touched his father's hand, and Ross Duncan's fingers closed over those of his son. Stuart knelt by the bed and kissed his father's cheek as he used to do when he was a small boy. The older man was evidently moved by the kindness, and a tear ran down his face.

"Come now," interrupted the doctor, more sternly than ever. "You would think the two of you hadn't seen each other for at least a year! We need to get your father ready for the operation, Stuart. You promised to help me and I need your full attention now."

The doctor soon had his patient as comfortable as possible under the circumstances. The case arrived, the gash was sewn up quickly, and by the end of the hour Ross Duncan was resting. The doctor had given him something to help him sleep, and was now talking with Stuart and Louise about the accident in another room.

Stuart Duncan's sister was very pretty, very proud, and very self-ish. She was six years younger than her brother and had been through two years of a finishing school in New York, but had not finished any particular area of study. She could play the piano and harp a little, and occasionally did some other things—but never housework. She was now lying on the sofa and began relating the story of the accident, while Stuart softly stroked her hair.

"Father and I started to drive down to the station this morning to meet you, Stuart. Since we were running early once we reached the road leading to the Forge mine, Father drove up to the engine house to handle some business. When we got up there, the miners were gathering to march down to the square. It was the first news of the strike we had heard. Father was very upset and began talking to the men—trying to persuade them to go back to work. Some of them talked back to him in a very insulting way, saying they were free men and didn't have to work for a corporation and things like that. You know how they talk, Stuart. Nothing makes Father more angry, and I don't blame him. I think these men are horrible to make so much trouble right now—just as I was getting ready to go back East for a cruise on a yacht with the Vasplaines. Now this strike will probably stop them from going.

"Anyway, then Father jumped down from the carriage and was about to physically confront one of the men who were insulting him. And that man deserved it too! But the others crowded around Father and forced him back into the carriage. I've never seen Father more angry, and I was nearly scared to death because the men were so rough. We drove back toward the main road, and near the sharp curve by the Beury mineshaft, we encountered another crowd of miners marching into town from the lower range of hills. They were carrying a large white banner with a horrible picture on it. The horses were frightened by the men and turned and ran right toward the old shaft.

"I don't know what happened then, except that we were thrown out of the carriage. It's a miracle I wasn't killed! Jem the coachman was driving and he fell onto a pile of ore. He ran up to the house, got the other horses, and brought Father and me home. I fainted several times, and when I saw Father lying on the bed with that awful gash on his head, I thought he was dead. If he does die, the miners will be to blame. If it hadn't been for their going out on strike, this horrible accident would never have happened. It's all as terrible as it can be!"

At that point Louise burst into tears and sobbed uncontrollably.

"My dear, you must have been hurt by the fall as well!" cried Stuart as he attempted to soothe and comfort her.

"No! I was not even bruised!" she replied. Louise then stopped crying, sat up on the sofa, and began to arrange her hair.

Dr. Saxon walked toward the other end of the room with a peculiar look on his face. He then wheeled around and said with his characteristic bluntness, "I need to get back to my office. I've left directions for your father's treatment. He is not seriously hurt, but send someone for me if you need to. Miss Louise, be sure to take these headache powders, and stay as quiet as possible today."

He laid the medicine on the table and left. A minute later his horse was heard galloping past the porch and down the road.

So that was what awaited Stuart Duncan at his homecoming after being abroad for a year. With great interest he had visited many of the famous capitals of Europe and had strolled through museums and art galleries. He had studied with genuine interest, although not in depth, the people he had met and the customs he had observed that were new to him. The year had been primarily a vacation for him, and he had spent money completely as he wanted—freely borrowing on his line of credit without giving it a second thought. After all, his father was a multimillionaire and was never stingy with his children. He wanted his son and daughter to have the best of everything from clothes to food to education to travel. Stuart had gone through Europe with the same carefree attitude he had experienced in college. He was in perfect health and had no vices, not even liking an occasional cigar. He would think deeply on some issues, but seemed to have no particular ambition or special interests. If he gave his future any thought while abroad, it was simply to picture a life of business in connection with his father's mining concerns. That was certainly his father's desire and Stuart had no argument to the contrary.

After returning home from the beautiful art galleries and cathedrals of the Old World, he was confronted with this terrible incident that had resulted in his father's injury. The miners' strike that had led up to the problem was especially personal to him, not only because it involved the Duncans' interests, but also because the strike leader was Eric Vassall, Stuart's boyhood playmate and lifelong friend. The more he thought about Eric, the more he realized the strike was a serious matter. Therefore, he and Eric might be greatly affected by it.

Nearly a week went by before Ross Duncan was able to sit up and talk much. During that time Stuart faithfully stayed home. He had not seen Eric, and Eric, as he supposed, had not been to see him. His father and Louise needed his constant care. But he felt a twinge of anticipation about seeing his old friend, especially whenever he thought of that scene in the public square and recalled Eric's prayer and its effect.

By the end of the week, father and son were talking together about the situation. The miners were still out on strike and there was no prospect of settlement.

"I tell you, Stuart," said Ross Duncan, while his large square chin became hard and tense, "the mining companies will never concede to the demands of the men! I will never move an inch toward them as long as they are on strike."

"Do you think the men are asking for too much, Father?"

"Too much! With ore at the present price! Just as we were beginning to get back on our feet, this is outrageous. We've had a very slow winter and things are just now starting to turn around again for us."

"But I thought ore had gone up. Isn't that what the men claim as the reason for their demand for an increase in pay? They say their wages ought to go up with the rise in the price of ore."

"They are fools!" Ross Duncan passionately struck the pillow beside him. "The companies were under contract for large quantities of ore at the old price before this rise came about. The increase will not benefit us at all until our old contracts expire."

"Then why don't the companies simply tell the men that?"

"Come on, Stuart! You are—" Ross Duncan restrained himself, albeit with great effort. Stuart was concerned for him and rose to move closer to the bed.

"Father, you must not get excited. Remember what Dr. Saxon said yesterday. Please don't talk any more about the strike."

"But I must! I will control myself."

It was wonderful to see the change that came over the man. He stiffened his muscles, then relaxed them, and let his hand, which had been clenched, open easily and lie open on the bed. Then he spoke without a hint of passion, slowly and coldly.

"The companies don't tell the men that because the men wouldn't believe a word the companies say. Yet there isn't a man in our mines who can say Ross Duncan ever cheated him out of a penny or ever told him a lie. I tell you, Stuart, the men are the most stubborn, ungrateful, ignorant lot of animals that ever lived. Last winter I kept more than a dozen families supplied with food and fuel for heat when they were sick and unable to work. I'd be willing to bet those very families are in the front row of the marchers every morning! These men are cutting their own throats. The companies will never give in to them."

Stuart did not say anything for a while. Then he said, "Don't you think, Father, that the men have been very self-controlled and law-abiding? There has been no real disturbance so far."

"Wait till we get the new men in from Chicago, and then let's see how they respond."

"Will the companies try to do that?"

"They certainly will if the strike continues another week. We will lose our contracts unless we can deliver the ore as agreed."

"Isn't it somewhat remarkable, Father," Stuart said, after another pause, "that the men have opened their meetings in the square every morning with prayer?"

Ross Duncan uttered a sound that expressed more contempt than a hundred words. "Who do they pray to? The devil?"

"The prayer I heard the first morning I got home was as good as any prayer I've ever heard in church."

"Who prayed it?"

"Eric," replied Stuart as his face slightly blushed.

"He is the leader of the whole strike—the most dangerous man on this range of hills today! I advise you to break off your friendship with him."

Stuart leaned forward a little. "You remember, Father, Eric saved my life when the elevator broke in the mineshaft?"

"Well, it was simply what anyone would do. You don't owe him any great debt."

Stuart did not reply. He began to feel a sense of the emotional passion and temper he had inherited from his father rising within him. Then after inquiring about his father's physical condition, he left the room.

That afternoon he walked up to the hills for the first time since his return. He sat down near one of the mines and thought through his talk with his father. Then he grew restless and walked down into the town. As he passed his office he went in and found a letter in the box addressed to him. He put it in his pocket, walked on through the square past the stage, crossed the railroad tracks, and went up the street. The street narrowed, as they all did, and became simply the miners' path. Finally, he reached a building belonging to another of his father's mines.

The pumps were still running, although some of the men had threatened to pull them out. There were only six men still at work in the engine house. Stuart walked on to his favorite seat on that hill—a large stone that jutted from the hillside. One of the few old pines still left on the slope grew nearby.

He sat down and took out the letter. It was from Eric. As he read, his face darkened.

"Dear Stuart"—the letter began with the old familiar greeting— "I'm writing you because I have been barred from entering your house. I dropped by twice this week and asked for you, but the servants would not let me in. I don't blame you. These difficult days are raising many issues, but the rights of these men cannot be ignored. I don't know if you even care to keep our friendship intact—that's up to you—and I don't know what the last year may have done to you. Perhaps this new situation may cause you to change your feelings toward me. Yet I am doing what I believe is right. From your perspective, however, it may appear all wrong. If you will be at the old stone by the big tree this afternoon, I will meet you there. Your old friend, Eric."

What Stuart had just read greatly troubled him, and Eric's being turned away from his house caused him to burn with rage. He could not understand it, unless the servants were acting under his father's orders. He turned red and then white-hot with anger at the thought. It was not like Ross Duncan to do such a thing. And yet, he might do it. The rest of the letter seemed unlike the old Eric he had known. Yet Stuart had more love for Eric than any other friend in his life. It was not because Eric had once saved his life, for he would have loved him in any case. But the years had brought changes—this past year in particular.

He had been reading and thinking through all this with his head bent down. As he raised it, he saw Eric coming up the hill.

The two friends greeted each other in the normal, commonplace way. "How are you, Eric?" "How are you, Stuart?" They shook hands stiffly and then sat down on the rock. Each seemed somewhat uncomfortable.

Stuart was the first to speak. He knew from experience that Eric would not say the first word. "I just finished reading your letter. Surely there is some mistake about your being turned away from my house. My father would never do such a thing, Eric."

"I'm not so sure of that. But I wouldn't feel hurt by that anyway, even if he did do it. Is he better?"

"Yes." Stuart paused. He did not seem to know what to say. It was much harder for him to bridge the last year away from Eric than he had expected. Then he burst out with a short laugh. "Eric, it is ridiculous for us to be sitting here like fools on this rock as if we were afraid of each other! For old time's sake, will you put your hand on my shoulder and look me in the eyes? Yet I know this is a different time, Eric." Stuart then sighed and let his own hand slip from Eric's shoulder.

"Yes, but I hope it's a better time. These days have made me sober and gray."

"How is that, Eric? Have your feelings toward me also changed?"

"No." Eric was pushing the gravel with his foot and looking out over the valley. Then he looked Stuart straight in the eyes and repeated, "No. You are really the one who has changed."

"I've changed! What change has there been in me?" Stuart asked the question almost indignantly.

"You have seen the world. What can I be to you now? And more and more, as time goes by, the difference will widen. You are a man of wealth and leisure, and I am a workingman."

"You don't have to be, Eric. You could get ahead. With your intellect you could command any place in life, and . . . and . . ."

Stuart hesitated for just the right word, but Eric said quietly, "I have chosen my place. I am a workingman, and I will be a workingman as long as there are wrongs to right and rights to maintain."

"But what does any of this have to do with our friendship, Eric? We've covered this ground before. Don't you love me?"

"Yes, I really do!" Eric turned his large, dark eyes affectionately toward his friend.

"And don't you know I love you?"

"Yes," replied Eric simply. "But by necessity our lives are being pulled farther apart. What is there to prevent it? It can't be helped because of the very nature of this present situation. Here I am advising thousands of men to take a course that is directly opposed by your father—and would be by you as well if you were in his place. The time is coming when the conflict between your interests and mine will be so fierce that—"

Stuart jumped to his feet. "Do you mean to say, Eric, that true and loving friendship cannot exist between you and me simply because of the accident of birth, or the circumstances of wealth, or difference in surroundings? Haven't we already proved that it can exist?"

"Yes," replied Eric slowly. "It can exist; but it is, in one sense, an unnatural existence. You represent money and management, while I represent labor. Take the present situation of this strike. I believe as much as I believe anything that it is right and even godly that we do what we are doing. Deeply, down in your heart, you condemn us for this action. If you were in your father's place, you would feel exactly as he does about it. How, then, can we expect the old relationship between us to continue?"

Stuart sat totally silent, looking out over the beautiful valley. The town looked quite pretty in its setting of hills and pines. His father's house was the most conspicuous residence in view. From where the two men sat it looked palatial. Down at the other end of the town, among the miners' houses, Stuart could just make out Eric's home. It was a little two-story cottage, like a hundred others. Stuart thought hard for several minutes and then said, "Eric, you began our discussion talking about the difference between us. Do you want to break off our friendship? Is that your intention?"

For the first time Eric became flushed across his dark, bronzed face. "No," he said. "I simply wanted to state the conditions under which we now live. There is no change in my feelings toward you, and there cannot be."

"Neither have my feelings for you changed, Eric. But why do you place all the responsibility totally on me, as if I will be the one to change, or as if the decision rests only with me to say whether or not our friendship is possible?"

"Because it does rest with you. Aren't you representative of riches, power, intelligence, leisure, culture, and all the great advantages and machinery that keep society in motion? And as a representative of all these things, shouldn't you bear the responsibility that must always rest on the strong, the educated, and the wealthy?" Eric then paused on the crest of the wave of his speech that seemed nearly to be breaking over his self-control.

After some time, Stuart doggedly remarked, "It comes back to this question: Will our friendship continue on the old basis? I can't change who I am. I have been born into wealth, leisure, education, society, and travel—and I am powerless to change it. And you are what you are because you have been born into it. You continue to live there only because you have chosen to do so, but you could rise above it if you only would."

"It is useless to discuss that point," replied Eric quietly. "But tell me, Stuart, getting back to the heart of the issue, do you believe in this strike?"

"No, I can't say that I do," Stuart said with his usual frankness.

"There! You see where the difficulty lies," replied Eric sadly. "The very nature of this situation demands a break in our old relationship with each other. Of course, I believe in the strike or I wouldn't be the leader of it."

"It seems to be a bad way to get what you want," said Stuart.

"Have you even studied the details of the situation? Do you know all the facts that have led up to this movement?"

"I know what my father has told me. He says the men did not consult with the companies and they went out without warning or notice of any kind."

Eric rose to his feet. "That's a lie!" he exclaimed with a sudden passion that no one would have suspected existed in him. It was like an explosion that transformed him into another being.

Stuart also rose. "Do you mean to say that my father lied to me about the facts?"

"I do!" retorted Eric. "He lied, and he knows he lied!"

Stuart took one step toward Eric, and the two young men confronted each other nose-to-nose. Eric turned on his heel and without a word walked down the hill. For a moment Stuart was on the verge of running after him or calling out to him to stop, but he stepped back to the stone and sat down. Once Eric had disappeared behind a clump of trees, Stuart stood and headed toward home down another path.

When he reached the house, Louise met him and told him their father wanted to see him at once. He went in and stood by the bed, while his entire being was still in turmoil over his conversation with Eric. The feeling was certainly not typical of his usually self-controlled nature. His father then began to speak with the bluntness that always characterized his speech.

"Stuart, I want you to go to Cleveland on business. This strike has caused complications with our local agents. There is important business that needs to be addressed in person. Can you go at once? The Eastern Express is due at six o'clock."

"I'm at your service, Father," replied Stuart. Yet he was still mentally reviewing his recent discussion with Eric.

"Here are the papers you will need. It will take only a few minutes for me to explain the business details to you."

Stuart pulled up a chair and his father gave him instructions. Then as Stuart put the papers in his pocket, Ross Duncan's face and manner seemed to soften somewhat. He fell back on his pillow and said, "Stuart, my son, in case anything happens to me, you know, of course, that I have left everything to you and Louise. The mines, surrounding property, the mining company funds, my New York property, and my personal bonds are worth more than four million dollars. I am leaving Louise one million dollars' worth of property, but you will be in charge of everything else when I die. Of course, you understand that I am the company. This strike is against me. And if I die, it will be against you. I believe I can depend on you to protect the millions of dollars I have worked so hard all my life to scrape together." Then reverting to his old stern manner, Ross Duncan said, "You will have to hurry to catch the train."

Stuart stood with conflicted feelings rising within him. What his father had just told him moved him in one way, while his afternoon with Eric moved him in another way. He felt compelled to ask his father just one question before he left.

"Father," he asked almost timidly, "did you tell me that the strikers walked out without giving the companies any notice or warning?"

"Yes."

"Do you mean that they gave absolutely no hint of their intentions to anyone?"

Ross Duncan rose up a little and his face changed. "They sent their representative, as they called him, to me about two weeks before the morning of the strike to discuss their wages. But I wouldn't recognize any such representative. They have no right to interfere with my business and tell me what wages I ought to pay."

"Who was the representative?" Stuart asked, already knowing the answer.

"Who was it? Only that praying, pious friend of yours, Eric Vassall!" Ross Duncan sat up, and the wound on his forehead turned purple. Stuart was frightened by the sight, but could not say anything. His father sank down in the bed again, exhausted by his anger. Stuart then left without uttering even one word of farewell. There was a bitterness in his heart that was new to him. Eric had been right after all. The company had received notice, and the workers had made an attempt to discuss the situation. As the train sped down the track, his heart cursed the complexities of the day's society.

He reached the city, attended to business, and started back the next day to Champion. It was dusk when he stepped onto the station platform. Seeing a crowd of curious onlookers, he knew something had happened. Dr. Saxon walked up, picked up Stuart's bag, and grasped his hand in a strong, but seemingly nervous way. Solemn and strangely sad faces looked out of the dusk at him.

"What's the matter, Doctor?" asked Stuart, suddenly trembling, but not knowing why.

"It's your father, my boy—"

"Is he worse?"

"Come this way. My buggy is right here and I will drive you out to your house. Get right in."

Stuart numbly climbed into the buggy. The doctor then jumped in, and the horse plunged into the darkness.

"Tell me the truth, Doctor." Stuart's voice was steady, but faint.

The answer came after a moment. "Your father died, Stuart—an hour ago. He had a stroke or sudden brain hemorrhage. There was also some heart trouble, but he did not suffer."

For a moment the entire universe seemed to be whirling around Stuart Duncan. Then he found himself asking questions, and Dr. Saxon was answering them. When they reached the house, Stuart saw Louise first. She came to the front door and threw herself into his arms, crying hysterically. Stuart had not shed a tear yet. They led him into the room where Ross Duncan lay. The son stood there, looking down at his father's cold face with that newly made scar on his forehead. He gave no thought to the fact that he was now the owner of several million dollars of wealth. He thought instead of his last conversation with his father and how he had departed without even a word of affection or good-bye. And still no tears of relief would come to him.

He walked from the room, and the sight of his sister's grief and fear brought the tears to his own eyes. He wept with her and they talked together. The doctor stayed another hour before leaving. As the night wore on, Louise, exhausted from the shock, went to her room. Stuart sent the servants away and was finally alone. He was unable to sleep, so he paced the long hallway until daylight. Just as the sun was rising, he went to look at his father again. Ross Duncan's millions were of no use to him now. Of what use would they be to his son? And what a load of responsibility had now come to him!

The mines, the labor problems, this strike, these wages—what difference would it make if he just walked away from it all? He had a right to do as he pleased with what he owned. He would sell the business and live abroad. He would . . . what! How could he be planning all this even before his father had been dead less than twenty-four hours? And what responsibility did fall to him? What difference did it make to him what wages the men received? Was he his brother's keeper? Were they his brothers? The whole thing seemed to be one complex irritant. His father's death had thrown a burden onto him that he did not want to carry.

A noise from the street in front of the house disturbed his thoughts. He went to the window and pulled the curtains open. The deliberate tramping of heavy feet could be heard coming down the road. Then a column of men four abreast came into sight, with one man somewhat out in front carrying a banner. The banner showed a crude drawing of a rich man and a poor man. The rich man was asking, "What do you want?" The poor man was responding, "Crumbs from your table." The message was certainly direct and very one-sided.

The column of men, nearly five hundred in number, marched by on their way from the upper range of hills to join the strikers in Champion during their regular morning gathering in the park. As each man passed by, he turned his head and looked up at the house where the mine owner lay dead. Perhaps they saw the son standing there. Stuart watched the entire group tramp through the dust and disappear down the road.

As he turned to look back toward the remains of the mortal flesh of the man who had been worth many millions of dollars, he was conscious that he stood face-to-face with the overwhelming problem of his own existence. And he knew his problem involved thousands of other men. How would he handle his dilemma?

2

great
responsibilities

A week after the death and burial of Ross Duncan, Stuart and Louise were talking together about their future plans. Louise lay on a sofa, looking very pretty and fashionable, although dressed for mourning. She appeared troubled by something Stuart had just said, and tapped her foot vigorously against the edge of the sofa.

"I'm losing patience with you, Stuart. Why don't you talk some sense?"

"I thought I was talking sense," replied Stuart, who was standing by one of the windows of the room looking out on the front lawn. He turned and walked back to the end of the room and continued to pace back and forth. He was deeply in thought, and part of the time seemed not to hear all that Louise said.

"You lose all your sense the minute the subject of these awful miners comes up," continued Louise. "If I were the governor of this state, I would order the militia out immediately."

"Why?" asked Stuart with a slight smile. "The men are not doing anything. What would you do with the troops?"

"I would get new men in to take the miners' jobs and then order the militia to protect them. And you know, Stuart, it's going to finally come to that."

Stuart did not respond. He was contemplating that very thing.

Louise went on talking while he stood still by the window for a minute looking out at the hills. "I regard Father's death as being caused directly by the miners. They frightened the horses and caused the accident that killed him. I don't see how you can side with the men in this strike."

"I'm not," Stuart said without turning around.

"Then why don't you do something to restart the mines? Don't we have a right to manage our own business and hire other men? And if the miners threaten to interfere, we also have a right to ask the governor for the state militia."

"I hope it will not come to that," replied Stuart gravely. He walked to the sofa and sat down by his sister. "Louise, I want to be totally honest and direct with you about this matter. I don't feel exactly like Father did about it."

"But you just said you didn't side with the men." Louise sat up and straightened her dress. Some ribbons near her collar kept her fingers busy for a minute.

"I don't side with them in the sense that I believe they are doing the right thing to strike this way. But I believe they ought to have more wages, and the companies ought to pay them the scale the miners have drawn up for themselves." Stuart was finally expressing his convictions out loud to his sister. They had been growing stronger within him ever since the day his father's death had thrown the burden of ownership upon him.

Louise received his words with a frown. She remained silent for a while, but then stood up and walked from the room. As she left, she angrily said, "Ross Duncan's son isn't much like his father. And you know it's true!"

Stuart stood and walked to the window again. He was upset—

not with Louise—but with the whole situation. Since his father's death he had gone through a great many struggles, and each one had left him with the feeling of even heavier responsibilities. No progress had been made with the strikers. In fact, the different mine owners had met in Cleveland and were united in their determination not to yield to the miners' demands for higher wages.

Stuart had been asked to attend another meeting in Cleveland this week, and he was planning to leave the next day. As he stood there looking out at the tree-covered hills, he knew that a crisis was rapidly approaching, and that the events of the next few days would forever leave their mark upon his entire life. He was not a coward, and that was the reason he could not run away from the situation. The interests of the mines in Champion were completely in his hands, but the other mines on the upper and lower ranges of hills were involved with his mines in the general strike. Therefore, he did not feel totally free to act alone. Besides, within a week of the walkout the men had formed a union and were now demanding recognition of the union as a whole and negotiations between the union and all the companies combined.

Meanwhile matters were coming to a crisis very fast. Stuart tightly clenched his fists and nervously bit his lip as he turned again from the window and paced the room. He was worth more than two million dollars in his own right, and yet possessing that much money caused him little real pleasure. He was having quite an inner struggle regarding the problem, and could not avoid feeling that before the week was over he would come face-to-face with the greatest challenge of his life.

While he stood there thinking, the doorbell rang. One of the servants came and said that Eric was at the door, so Stuart walked into the hall.

"Come in, Eric," he said quietly.

Eric stepped inside, and the two young men shook hands

silently before sitting down to talk. Since Ross Duncan's death they had met several times, and it seemed as if the old friendship between them might be possible again. There was, however, still a serious barrier caused by the issues surrounding them.

"I came here this morning," began Eric with his usual directness, "to tell you that the men want you to speak to them at the park today at noon."

Stuart was surprised. "I thought the men would not allow anyone on the stage unless he was one of the miners."

"They haven't so far. You are the only one, or you will be, if you come to the meeting today."

"What do the men want?" Stuart asked, not really sure that he cared to go.

Eric did not reply immediately. He seemed to be waiting for Stuart to say something more. Stuart just sat there looking at Eric with that strange, quiet gaze of his. "Do the men want me to make a speech regarding this current struggle?"

"I don't know exactly what they expect. They simply voted to ask you to come today at noon. It may be an opportunity for a settlement." Eric spoke slowly, while Stuart suddenly stood and placed a hand on his old friend's shoulder.

"Eric," he said, while a sad smile crossed his face and died out into its usual thoughtful quiet, "doesn't it seem strange to you that such a big problem has arisen over the difference of a few cents more pay for a day's work? Is life really worth living if we have to spend it on such serious battles over such trivial matters?"

"You call this a trivial matter?" Eric responded almost bitterly. And then he bluntly added, "Perhaps a few cents a day is trivial to a man who has plenty of money, but it may mean the difference between comfort and suffering for a man who has almost nothing."

Stuart's face reddened, but he quietly answered, "No, Eric, you are not understanding me. I am ready to pay the difference in the men's wages. I think their demand is just."

"Then come to the park at noon and tell them so."

"Well, I will. By the way, I want you to know that I am going to Cleveland tomorrow, Eric."

"If the other owners there were like you, the strike would not last very long," said Eric as he stood to leave. He had a great deal to do to prepare for the noon meeting, so in spite of Stuart's urging him to stay longer, he left. Yet there was still a wedge between the two of them. They were not comfortable in each other's presence. Eric had not mentioned their first meeting again, and while Stuart now felt differently about it, he had not spoken with Eric about it either.

Stuart told Louise of his invitation to speak to the men at the park and went outside sometime later, intending to go into the hills to think all alone. But as he drove out onto the road he changed his mind and went down into the town, stopping at Dr. Saxon's office. He thought he would ask his advice on the matter.

The doctor was alone, which was rare for him. He jokingly greeted Stuart in a way that only a lifelong friend could do. "Well, you aristocrat! Are you going to continue trampling on the poor downtrodden masses much longer? Are you going to continue to withhold their rightful wages from them?"

Ignoring the doctor's attempt at humor, Stuart flatly stated, "Doctor, I'm going to speak to the men in the park at noon today."

"You are? Well, give 'em a dose of their own medicine . . . enough to put 'em on the sick roll for a month. They're the most ungrateful, obstinate, pigheaded, senseless crowd of human animals I've ever seen! I've made up my mind, Stuart, not to do another thing for 'em. Anyway, ever since the strike started I've not been paid by the mining companies to help them."

"No, I suppose you're right. Your contract with the mines is good only while the mines are in operation."

"Even so, these wild Cornishmen expect me to doctor 'em whether I'm being paid for it or not. And I've made up my mind that I won't do it any longer."

At that moment there was the sound of shuffling footsteps outside, followed by a thump on the door that sounded as if it were made by the thick end of a club.

"Come in!" shouted the doctor. "Here's one of 'em now," he said to Stuart in a quiet voice. "Watch me deal with him."

The door opened and a man of enormous build shuffled into the room. He had a massive head of tangled yellow hair, and his beard was the same color. He was at least six feet four inches in height, and his arms and feet were astonishingly long. Stuart leaned back into the window seat to watch, and although he was somewhat preoccupied with what he was going to say to the men, he couldn't help but smile at the scene that followed.

"I've come to get my medicine bottle filled, Doctor," the miner quietly remarked.

The doctor did not move at all to take the bottle that the man had pulled from his vest pocket. The miner stood there, awkwardly holding it in both hands.

"Well, you can just get out of here with your bottle, Sanders. I'm not refilling any bottles anymore."

"Since when?" asked Sanders slowly.

"Ever since this strike . . . this ridiculous and foolish strike of yours and the others. Do you really think I'm going to go to all the expense of continuing to stock all these drugs and medicines, stitch you fellows up, and supply you with costly remedies, while I'm not getting anything from the companies? So get out of here with your bottle!"

Sanders silently backed toward the door. The doctor wheeled around toward his desk and began to hum a tune. But just as the miner laid his hand on the doorknob, the doctor turned his head and shouted, "What was in that bottle, anyway!"

"Cod-liver oil," replied Sanders, scratching his head and slowly turning the doorknob.

"When did you get it filled?"

"Last week, sir."

"Last week! It was three days ago, or I'm a striker. What on earth did you do with half a pint of cod-liver oil in that short amount of time?"

Sanders shook his head and smiled faintly, but did not venture to say anything.

"Have you been shining your boots with it? I'd be willing to swear that you have—only half a pint wouldn't oil more than one of 'em. Well, bring it here! I'll refill it just once and that's all. What did I give it to you for, anyway? Do you remember?"

Sanders kept discreetly silent as the doctor said to Stuart, "It isn't cod-liver oil exactly. It's a new preparation that I have just had sent up from Chicago, and it has been of some help in lung ailments. Perhaps I'll let him have another bottle. He has a bad cough." As if to second the doctor's statement, Sanders hoarsely coughed. The rumble from it seemed as deep as the man was tall, and it shook the bottles on the doctor's medicine shelves. The doctor measured out the man's medicine, grabbed a new cork, and as he handed the bottle over, cheerfully said, "Sanders, I know you will forget everything I'm going to tell you, but you must remember that if you don't follow the directions on this bottle, you are liable to fall down dead any minute. Now, is there anything else?"

The miner was slowly fumbling through a lot of loose change in his pocket. "How much is this?" he finally asked.

"Oh, well, that's all right," said the doctor, turning red. "Keep it to remember me by. Consider it a birthday present from me. But mind you, no more medicine from this office till the strike is over. I can't afford to doctor a thousand men for nothing."

Sanders left as the doctor turned to Stuart and said, "I thought I might as well let him have it. Shoot! I'm too easy. But Sanders has tuberculosis. It's awfully strange how so many of these big fellows catch it."

Suddenly, there was another tap on the door, and before the doctor could answer, the door opened and a little old woman came in. She had a very sad face and looked like one of those people who know life mainly from its troubles.

"Doctor," she said, after nodding to Stuart, "me old man is sufferin' terrible this mornin'. I want ya to send him somethin' to ease the pain a bit."

"Where is his pain?"

"Huh?"

"I said, 'Where is his pain?' In his head or feet?"

"In his back, Doctor. An' he's howlin' like murder for somethin' to ease it. I come right down here. He said, 'The doctor will give me anythin' I need.'"

"Yeah, that's it! These beggars don't care if I go into bankruptcy and ruin by giving them anything they need."

The doctor stood again and walked over to his medicine shelves. After a very careful search he selected a bottle and poured from it into a small one. He jotted down some directions, pasted them on the bottle, and gave the medicine to the woman.

"There now, Mrs. Binney, I know just what your husband's trouble is. He strained the muscles of his back that time he tried to lift those timbers in the DeMott mine."

"Yes." The woman's face lit up with pride. "Jim held up the timbers until the other men crawled out."

"That's true, which is why I don't mind helping him. Use this as I have directed and it will give him some relief."

The woman thanked the doctor, and as she turned to go, she wiped her eyes with her sleeve. The doctor followed her out into the hall, and Stuart could not help hearing him say to her, "Tell Jim I'll be out to see him this afternoon, Mrs. Binney."

The doctor walked back into the office, and as he sat down at his desk, he slammed it with his fist. "That's the last case I'll take till this strike ends! The only way to bring these people around is to treat them sternly. I tell you, Stuart, I can't afford to go on giving away medicine and service this way. It will ruin me, and besides, it isn't professional."

There was a timid knock at the door, so the doctor picked up a medical magazine and turned his back to the door. He pretended to read, but was holding the magazine upside down. After the doctor ignored another rap on the door, it swung open. A boy about twelve years old timidly walked in and stood with his cap in his hand. He looked first at Stuart and then at the doctor's back.

"My father's been hurt. He's the pump man at the Davis mine. He wants you to come right up!"

"Up where?" asked the doctor without turning around.

"Up where we live."

"Where's that?"

"The same place."

"What's his name?"

"Why, you know his name, Doctor. You've seen him before."

The doctor wheeled around and roared, "Well! I can't be expected to know the names of a thousand different men! Who is your father?"

"He's the pump man in the Davis mine."

"Well, six different pump men are up there. Which one is he?"

The boy began to get scared and backed toward the door.

"What's the matter with your father?" asked the doctor more gently, rising and reaching out for his black case and putting on his hat.

The boy began to sob. "I don't know. He's hurt."

"Well, you run down and get into my buggy and sit there till I come. Hurry now!" The boy backed out of the door and rumbled down the stairs. The doctor gathered up his things, and while shouting to Stuart, "This case seems to call for my help," he dashed out of the room.

There was a drugstore directly under the doctor's office, where he kept a case of candy. Stuart, leaning out of the window, saw the doctor come out of the store with a bag of something that he gave to the boy. Then, getting into the buggy, he took off at his usual rapid pace and disappeared in a huge whirlwind of red iron-ore dust.

Stuart smiled and said to himself, "Dear old Doc! I was thinking that his bark was worse than his bite . . . only it's all bark." But his face turned serious again as he saw a sight from the window that was becoming quite familiar to the people of Champion.

It was now about eleven o'clock, and in the open space around the stage in the center of the town square the miners were beginning to cluster into groups of two to four men or so. They came from their homes out in the hills. Each miner was carrying a stick, the purpose of which became more apparent as the men began to line up in marching columns.

Several different mines' brass bands had already assembled near the stage. They joined together to play some stirring songs while the crowd was gathering. The square filled up very quickly. Finally, as the clock on the tower pointed its hands to a quarter after eleven, four thousand men were packed into the open square surrounded by the town buildings. Stuart continued to look and listen from the doctor's office window while the entire scene played out before him.

Several times since the day of his return from his European trip he had seen the miners gather like this, but today he was impressed more than ever by the appearance of the men. He noticed their crudely made, misspelled banners and listened to the music played entirely by men from the mines, who with great patience had learned to play march tunes. But more than anything else, he was struck by the faces of the men, and the somewhat unemotional, yet determined look that most of them portrayed. He was also impressed by the simple fact that these human beings would fight for their right for a few more cents per day. Through all of this he could not help feeling that the men regarded him as an aristocrat, far removed from them his entire life. His life was very different from theirs, and at least from their point of view, it caused him to be unable to sympathize with or understand them.

"And yet," Stuart said to himself with a sigh, "I would nearly trade places with almost any one of them. What I mean is that I am not in a position to use what I have been born with and inherited as I would like."

The bands stopped playing, and a miner walked up to the stage. All the men removed their hats, and it became very quiet. The people of Champion stood looking on from the sidewalks, the church steps, the railroad station platform, and the store and office windows. The man on the stage looked toward heaven and offered a short prayer.

"O God, grant us a blessing today as we meet together. Be with us as we consult with one another. Grant that we may be led to do what is right. Keep us all from any trespass, sin, or drunkenness. And once we have ended the striving of this life here below, may we all—Master and men—meet in heaven. We ask this in Jesus' name. Amen."

Stuart heard every word of the prayer from where he sat. There was something indescribably sad to him in the whole scene. The miners put on their hats and the bands quickly struck up a lively tune. The men began to move out onto the main street, forming a double line four abreast. Each section of the line had a band marching before it. When signaled to do so, the men shouldered their sticks, and having now become accustomed to marching, they presented quite a military appearance as they swung past the church and onto the road leading over to the park where they now held their daily meeting at noon.

Stuart watched for Eric, and as he came by, he called to him from the window, "I'll drive over. My horse and buggy are here."

Eric waved his hand and marched by without replying. Stuart walked down, and after the columns of men had passed, he drove along a short distance behind them.

All the way there he debated what he would say. It was the first time he had really faced the men, and many of them had no idea of the feelings of the new mine owner. They believed that Ross Duncan's son must be just like his father. Yet some among them had known him since he was a child and liked him. He was actually one of the favorites of the townspeople. Many a rough, reckless, and strong Dane and Cornishman admired him as a young man who had been so fearless working in the mining shafts. And a number of favorable comments were being made among the men regarding his coming to speak with them today.

After finally reaching the park, he was met by a committee of the men and escorted to the speaker's pavilion. He faced quite a large crowd, but one that at least was prepared to give him a fair hearing. More than a thousand men had traveled from some of the other ranges of hills, bringing the audience to more than five thousand who were crowded around the pavilion.

Later Stuart would be unable to remember exactly what he or the others had said. Eric spoke briefly, and then on behalf of the recently formed union, he explained that he had the pleasure of introducing the owner of the Champion mines, who would address the meeting.

Stuart had never spoken in public except on a few occasions in college classes. He was no orator and he knew it. And although he was in a position that might have been quite stressful to even experienced speakers, as he stood to address this outdoor gathering, he felt a sense of relief and pleasure.

He began by immediately stating his willingness to grant the men their wage demands. "If I understand the situation," he said, "the demand made by the contract miners is for two dollars a day due to the danger of the work, and due to the fact that the mining companies have been paying just one dollar and ninety cents for more than a year. I believe the companies should grant this demand. I must say, however, that I do not agree with the course you have chosen to get what you want. I cannot sympathize with your strike, but I do sympathize with your demand for two dollars per day."

"What about the rest of the companies?" someone asked.

"Yeah! What about those on the lower range of hills? What's your thinking on them?" yelled another.

"I can't answer for them. I am here today to speak only for myself. If the men who are employed in the Champion mines will return to work, I will give them what they ask."

Stuart's statement was greeted with cheers. But a storm of protests arose from all around the park. "All or none!" they cried.

"The union comes first!"

"The owners must deal with the union!"

"We'll never go back on terms that shut others out!"

"Stand together, men! That's what the owners do."

"Yes! They fix wages and we'll fix them if—"

Eric stood up and waved his hat. There was a gradual settling down of the confusion, and as he stood there, evidently waiting to be heard, the men soon became quiet again. Stuart admired his control of the crowd, for Eric had great influence with them.

"Brothers," he said slowly, "I believe we have reached a critical point in this movement. Here is one of the owners who has expressed his willingness to grant our demands. The question now is: Will the Champion men go back to their mines while the rest continue to deal with the other owners? This is a question for the union to settle."

"Eric," Stuart said in a quiet voice since he stood close by him, "please allow me to say a word or two more. I believe the decision of these men today is a serious one, and I want to do all I can to make it right."

Eric quickly raised his voice. "Men, Mr. Duncan wants to say another word. I'm sure you will give him a fair and careful hearing."

"Yes, that we will."

"He's not bad for a millionaire."

"Give him a chance. He doesn't often have it!" shouted a voice with a touch of irony in it.

Stuart took advantage of the lull that followed these and other shouts to speak as he had never dreamed of doing when he first arrived at the park. He believed that the consequences of the men's decision would be exceedingly important for them and for him. And he had never had such a strong desire to express his feelings regarding the struggle between labor and management, and how it affected him.

It is impossible to describe his speech. Eric thought at the time that it was the best speech he had ever heard from a man of wealth. At times it was filled with passion, but then quiet and conversational. Yet it is doubtful very many of the miners totally understood exactly what Stuart meant. In reality, he was directing his words to men of wealth, and he intended to follow through by encouraging them to change their ways.

This much he made clear to the men: he sympathized with their demands for better wages, while he could not agree with their methods. Also, he would do everything in his power to grant them their just demands insofar as he was free to act independently of the other owners. He told them, in fact, that he was going to Cleveland the next day to meet with the other mine owners, and that he would use all his influence to get them to agree to the rise in wages. He then repeated his offer to deal fairly with the thousand or more men employed in the Champion mines whenever they chose to return. As he closed, he made an appeal to the men to use reason, and he spoke of the religious influence that so far had prevailed for the good of the community.

Through his entire speech ran an underlying, yet passionate, desire to be understood as a man before men. He had never before had such a longing to be understood, nor had he ever felt the gap between himself and the men to be so wide and deep. Nevertheless, it is doubtful that certain parts of his speech were understood at all by the men.

As soon as he finished there was a great uproar of applause and shouts. Even Eric could not restore quiet. The committee politely asked Stuart to leave the park while the union went into conference to discuss his proposals. Stuart was glad to leave, feeling quite exhausted from the draining experience.

It was three o'clock in the afternoon when Eric came to the house with the news of the decision reached by the miners' union. Stuart immediately saw by the look on Eric's face that the situation was serious.

"The men voted by a large majority not to go back to work until all the miners could return under the same terms. Essentially, they demanded that all the mine owners recognize the union and deal with it for all the men at the same time."

"Do you mean to say that the men who work in the Champion mines refuse to accept my offer of the wages they demand?"

"Yes. That is, the Champion miners will not go back until the other owners grant the same terms you have, and do so with the union."

"Which simply means that this strike is a deadlock," replied

Stuart decidedly. "I know the men in Cleveland, and they will never agree to any such terms."

"The miners will not agree to any other terms either." Eric spoke quietly but sadly.

"Eric," said Stuart suddenly, after a pause, "tell me frankly, as brother to brother, is this a reasonable step for the men to take? Do you believe the union will succeed by taking such an action? Is it just and fair?"

Eric's face revealed true passion. Then he said, "The men have a right to unite for mutual support. In this instance they feel driven to it by their plight. Why shouldn't labor seek to defend itself just as management does? You, that is, I mean the mine owners generally, get together as a group and fix wages. Why shouldn't the miners get together and have their say about it? We have been working for years for a wage set by men from a distance, who have never seen a mine or a miner, and who have never gone underground to see what the work entails. These men sit in nice, leather-upholstered offices in elegant buildings and make it their business to get just as much out of the iron ore as they can, while the wages of the men are cut every time ore falls in price. Instead of taking it out of their own large dividends in the years when they have made enormous profits, they cut on this end instead of their own every time there is a drop in the market. And you know it's true, Stuart.

"Just three years ago a dozen men in the iron industry grew to be millionaires from the profits of this metal that God put in the ground for the common use of all. During that year the miners received only fair wages. Since then, financial depression and the drop in the price of ore have followed. So what do those men do who have in prosperous years made their fortunes? Do they say, 'We will draw on our reserve, and in order that the miners may not suffer we will declare smaller dividends and lose something ourselves'?

No! They quickly say, 'Let's cut wages because ore is cheaper and we can't afford to lose.'

"So who suffers? Not the mine owners! They eat just as well, go to Europe on their steamships, drive their elegant carriages, and enjoy their many hobbies. But the poor man, to whom every cent means something, goes without the basic necessities of life. And his wife and children suffer because the millionaire who made his fortune on his business is not willing to share a part of it during hard times with the men who made his wealth possible through their labor. I tell you, Stuart, my heart is on fire for this cause, yet no one knows how the working men in this country feel unless he has been one himself. As for the union, it is an organization that has sprung up from the wrongs that are simply devilish in their human selfishness."

Stuart sat with his head bowed during Eric's speech. Then he said gently, "And what if the union develops the same kind of selfishness in the workingmen? Then what?"

"Then the workingmen will suffer. It will be inevitable."

"And what if the mine owners decide to hire new men for the mines?"

"Then there will be trouble."

"Do you mean that you will incite the men to violence?"

"Heavens no! Stuart, you know I won't. I will use all my power to prevent anything of the kind."

"But what if it cannot be prevented?"

Eric said nothing. His face changed from the torrent of feeling and passion he felt. "If it comes to that, let God judge if the owners, and not the men, are really the ones most to blame. I will use all my influence to prevent violence or lawlessness. The union has a right to unite for wages it believes are just. But it has no right to prevent other men from working at any wage they choose to take. Ever since I joined the Salvation Army I have become convinced that the only permanent basis for any true settlement of disputes between labor and management must be a true religious basis— that is, a Christian basis."

Stuart listened with genuine interest. "How did you happen to join the Salvation Army, Eric?"

"It's a long story. I'll tell you some day, but not now."

"I've heard part of it, but I want you to tell me all of it."

"I can't now. I have to go. I've hardly had a minute's time to myself since this movement began. I have to leave now. You leave for Cleveland when?"

"Tonight. I want to be there tomorrow. But I can tell you now what the companies will say. Is there no other way out of this?"

"I don't see any," replied Eric.

The two men shook hands silently, and Eric left.

Stuart traveled on the night express train, and the next day at Cleveland was in conference with the other owners. The result of the conference was what he had anticipated, for the terms of the union were rejected. The owners also decided that a force of men should be hired to operate the steam shovels to move the stockpiles of ore, and that in case there was trouble, the troops should be called out. But Stuart refused to take this action in his own mines, not yet wanting to replace his workers on the stockpiles or in the mines. He returned home the following day with a feeling of indecision and to a time of waiting. He could not sympathize with the strike, and he did not believe the union was wise in refusing to let the Champion miners go to work. And he could not help feeling that a great calamity lay ahead.

Just two days after his return, the event occurred that really shaped and molded the remainder of his life. The mines were still manned by pump men. They had not been called out on strike by the union for the simple reason that if the water in the mines rose above a certain level and began to soak the timbers, the mines would be ruined. The resulting loss would then be as great for the miners as for the owners. In this way, once the strike ended, work could easily resume. Six to eight men remained at each mine: an engineer, an assistant, one or two firemen, and three or four pump men—depending on the mine's size and the number of pumps. The pumps ran day and night because the water rose very rapidly if allowed to collect.

Stuart had gone up to the Davis mine, one of the new ventures of his father and just recently developed. Its greatest depth was nine hundred feet. It had a manhole with ladders, and a shaft some distance away from it for the "skip," or iron carriage, used for hauling ore to the surface. Six men were on duty at the mine at the time.

Stuart had gone to the engine house and was talking with the engineer when Eric came in. Stuart called him over to the "dry room"—the place where the miners put on their work clothes.

"Eric, I want to go down into the mine. Will you go with me? I want to see again for myself what the work entails, and besides, there is a new pump at the bottom I would like to see."

Eric consented, and the two soon had on miners' outfits and were headed down the ladders. It was getting late in the afternoon, and they left orders with the engineer that when they gave the signal from the bottom, he should lower the skip so they could ride it back to the top.

They explored the different levels of the mine for an hour. Stuart seemed restless, and was intent on learning as completely as possible exactly how the miners worked. He climbed into difficult places, and even set off a blast in one chamber, using one of the explosive sticks left by the men when they walked out.

Finally, he and Eric stood at the very bottom of the mine. The area was an excavation about fourteen feet across, and water ran into it as if it were a cistern. By leaning back against the ladders, they could see the light from nine hundred feet above. Eric was sitting with his back to the ladder rungs, dangling his feet in the water, which covered the floor of the mine to a depth of about four inches. Meanwhile, Stuart was examining the pump at the other side of the shaft when something terrible happened.

They heard a roar like that of a severe storm headed right for them. Before Eric could jump from his seat on the ladders, a massive amount of iron ore came crashing down the manhole, knocking out rungs of the ladders as it fell. The ore bounced from side to side, finally striking Eric on his shoulders with tremendous force, slamming him facedown into the water.

Stuart rushed to his side, picked him up, and with the light of the candle in his hat, began to assess the situation. He could not tell whether the ore had fallen or had been purposely thrown into the shaft. He dragged Eric away from the foot of the ladder, and realized he was seriously injured. With only one thought—that of getting Eric to the top as soon as possible—Stuart grabbed the lever at the bottom of the ore shaft and pulled it back, attempting to signal the engineer to lower the skip. There was no return signal, so Stuart pulled once more. Still no answer. He heard a clanking sound followed by quiet. The pumps had stopped. As he looked up through the main shaft, he saw a bright light at the top. But what was it? It couldn't be the sun. It must be nearly sundown by now. Something was on fire!

He was struck with the terrifying truth that the engine house over the main shaft was on fire! The ladders were a possible way of escape, but certainly not for someone attempting to carry a body—and perhaps a dead one at that. Stuart splashed water in Eric's face, causing him to groan. He was not dead, but unconscious. Then the total gravity of the situation forced its way into Stuart's mind. He was a prisoner with a helpless, wounded man, and they were trapped at the bottom of a mine nine hundred feet deep. The engine house was on fire, which prevented the lowering of the skip.

The pumps had stopped, and the water in the mine was already halfway to his knees.

He pulled the lever again and again, and in his excitement he shouted like a madman. There was no answer from above. The manhole ladders were still safe from the fire. So even with the many broken rungs, because he was young and strong, he would be able to climb out. But it would be impossible to carry Eric out as well!

Suddenly, a charred fragment of wood floated down the ore shaft, hissing as it dropped into the water. Realizing he was standing in the presence of death, Stuart offered a prayer for help. He clung to Eric, holding him the best he could. Meanwhile the water was above his knees and rapidly rising.

3

the rescue

As the facts surrounding his situation forced themselves more clearly upon him, but with the initial excitement over, Stuart began to calm down somewhat. The candle in his hat was nearly burned out, but he had another one. He had done what miners typically do—tucked another candle into his boot when he had changed clothes in the dry room. He pulled it out, lit it, and placed it into the candleholder of his hat, replacing the stub of the first one.

Then he carefully looked at the ladders. The massive chunk of ore that had fallen down the manhole had broken out a dozen rungs at the very bottom of the ladder. But by stretching to his full height, Stuart could just reach an unbroken one.

But how could he handle the dead weight of Eric? He could never lift him up that distance. For just one fleeting second, Stuart considered the thought of leaving Eric. It was simply his love for life asserting itself. Why should both of them die? His death would not save Eric. He pondered the idea for only a moment and then felt the shock of his thoughts. He knew life would not be worth living if he had to carry these memories forever. He could never abandon the man who had once risked his life to save him and had done so when the danger was just as great as now. "But, O God," Stuart cried out, "to drown like a rat in a hole!"

He felt his love for life rising within his being, just as the water continued to rise even more rapidly. It was nearly to his waist. He held Eric's unconscious body as comfortably as possible, and he felt the blood from the wound in Eric's shoulder warming his own side. Occasionally, Eric moved a little, and once he opened his eyes, so Stuart mistakenly thought he was regaining consciousness. If only he could regain enough strength to help even a little! Stuart's mind whirled as he thought of possible ways to pull himself and Eric up the ladder a short distance. But the bottom of the mine offered no rocky projections or ridges with which to gain a foothold.

The fire at the top was evidently blazing fiercely. Fragments of charred wood continued dropping down the ore shaft. Leaning over and looking up, Stuart could see a huge flaming mass of twisted beams and iron rods curling over the mouth of the shaft. He moved directly under the manhole, dragging Eric with him, and looked up. The flames and smoke were sweeping over it like mist over a ridge. Even from a distance of nine hundred feet, he thought he could see the ladders near the top blazing out of control.

He gave up all hope. Yet with the basic survival instinct still strong, he dragged Eric over to the pump, which stood above the water level. Mustering all his strength, he managed to place Eric on it so that he was two or three feet above Stuart as he stood on the floor of the mine. The water had risen to nearly shoulder level and was whirling around him like a large red pool. He shuddered because it looked just like blood under the light of his candle. Moving Eric in this way, plus contact with the cold water, had finally awakened him. He stirred slightly and even spoke, although feebly.

"Where are we?" he muttered.

"You have been hurt, Eric."

Eric groaned and closed his eyes. Then he opened them again, and the sight of Stuart's pale face seemed to tell him some of the truth of their situation. The water was now running over the hand of his right arm, which helplessly hung from his wounded shoulder. He raised himself somewhat, but evidently with great difficulty.

"You will drown. Leave me. I am dying anyway."

"No! No! Eric, I will not leave you here alone!" Stuart spoke firmly but somewhat calmly and nearly cheerfully. Eric's face dropped close to Stuart's shoulder. Stuart kissed Eric's cheek, and at that very moment he heard a man's voice. Echoing down the ladder shaft, it was the sweetest sound he had ever heard.

He shouted a reply and then waited. Again a cry came in response. Someone was coming down the ladders to the rescue. Whoever it was, he was descending quickly in spite of the condition of the ladders. Stuart heard words of encouragement, and then a voice spoke from the last rungs of the ladder that were intact. In very distinct and precise English, he heard, "Who is there?"

"It is I, Stuart Duncan. I am here with Eric, and he is hurt and helpless. I can't lift him up alone."

"I always believed in being on time," replied the voice. "If you can move under the foot of the shaft, I will throw you this rope."

Stuart lifted Eric from the pump and then plunged toward the ladder shaft. The water was now above his shoulders. A rope was thrown to him and he tied it around Eric, who had again fainted from the pain and shock. Then with all the strength and skill that men possess only when facing death, the two men, one above and one below, succeeded in lifting Eric. The man above secured Eric, while Stuart, using the sides of the ladder for support, pulled himself from the watery grave.

The maneuver happened not a minute too soon, for the water was flowing in more rapidly. The large area at the bottom of the shafts was completely filled, and the torrent of water was rising even faster in the shafts themselves. There was no time to ask any questions of the rescuer, for all three men were in great danger. The ladders were blazing above them, and the water was rising below them. With superhuman effort they began lifting Eric. When they came to rungs that were badly broken, they had to be extremely careful to safely continue with him. They took so long at one point to start moving again that Stuart, who was at the bottom, again felt the torrent of water swirling around his feet.

Finally, after a struggle that had left them completely exhausted, they reached the first drift, or horizontal passageway, from the bottom. A wooden platform was there, and the drift ran out into the sides of the hill several hundred feet. Stuart and his unknown rescuer leaned against the side of the wall panting, while Eric lay on the platform, appearing lifeless.

"We can't stay here long," gasped Stuart. "See the water coming up!" He pointed down the black well from which they had climbed so painfully. The rushing water and the pieces of ore continuing to fall around them made a terrifying roar.

"We can get out on this level," replied his companion.

"What! How can we? We're still eight hundred feet below ground level."

"The old Beury shaft opens into this drift. I walked in here this afternoon. This is where I heard you shout for help. There! Don't you feel that breeze blowing through the drift?"

Stuart turned his face and felt the passing of cool, flowing air. Then he remembered that years ago, when he was just a boy, he had climbed into the old Beury shaft that opened up on the side of the hill. And he had also made his way to the level of the Davis mine—to the very point where he now stood. Mines were sometimes connected in that way, although the abandoned passageways often became blocked by collapsing walls of ore.

There was still no time to lose, even with the unexpected avenue of escape. The two men picked up Eric and hurried as quickly as their burden would allow, following the passage that connected the main shaft with the deserted one. After they walked about two hundred feet, the drift turned abruptly to the right and began to ascend sharply. It became more difficult to carry Eric, but at least the danger from the water was over. The old passage was really a tunnel drilled into the side of the hill at a sharp incline, instead of a shaft sunk vertically from top to bottom. Once they were sure they were safely beyond the reach of the water, they sat down exhausted again. Then by the flickering candlelight, Stuart finally realized who his rescuer was.

"I do not have any business cards with me, but allow me to introduce myself," he said in a way that made Stuart smile. Yet there was nothing flippant or lacking in seriousness about the man. "I am the new minister at the church with the clock tower—St. John's. I arrived in Champion two days ago. My name is Andrew Burke. Aren't you Mr. Duncan, the mine owner? I am glad to meet you."

He held out his hand and Stuart took it, shaking it above Eric, who lay between them. He felt a strange sensation as he shook the minister's hand. For some reason the peculiar formality of the man's speech struck him as a sign of a special kind of strength. He seemed to feel that here was a man who, despite his peculiarities, possessed qualities that were quite rare and valuable.

"I owe you my life, and that of my friend here," Stuart said. "Your showing up here seems very strange to me. I had given myself up for lost. I would certainly have drowned if you had not appeared."

"Yes, I believe you would have. That is, unless you had left your friend down there. But you don't look like the kind of man who would do that. We should move on now. We need to get him to the doctor as soon as possible. My showing up here is quite simple—I will explain later. Shall we move on?"

Stuart eagerly agreed, so they stumbled on up the tunnel. Their progress was very slow, for Eric was like a dead weight, and neither Stuart nor his rescuer was a physically powerful man. They had gone just a short distance, however, when lights appeared farther up the shaft, and soon they were surrounded by a group of miners accompanied by Dr. Saxon.

There was no time for more than the briefest explanation. The rescue party took Eric from Stuart and the minister, and they were soon standing outdoors on the side of the hill under the stars. The cool night air blew around Stuart, and he thanked God for life. Farther up the hill a heap of blazing ruins marked the place where the engine house had stood, while a short distance from it the ladder hole smoked and flamed like a small volcano, showing that the timbers were still fiercely blazing below.

"Take Eric to my house. We're not far from it," Stuart said.

"Yes, and hurry up, men!" added the doctor. "I'll go on ahead with them, Stuart. Eric needs attention as soon as possible."

The doctor and the miners with Eric hurried down the hill, while Stuart followed with the minister as fast as he could. But now that all the stress had ended he felt weak and faint.

"You must stop in and visit with me tonight, Reverend Burke. I want to know the story behind your showing up at the mine. Besides, I've not had time to properly thank you."

"I will be glad to accept your invitation. In fact, I would like to wash up before returning to town. I'm staying at the hotel," replied Burke.

As the two walked along, carefully choosing every step down a narrow path, a strange noise wafted up from town. Stuart paused to listen.

"What's that?" he asked.

"Troops. They arrived this afternoon. That must be the drumbeat calling them to quarters."

"I didn't expect them until the end of the week. At least, that's what I was told in Cleveland."

"They came this afternoon, and I imagine that's one reason for your friend's injury. We'll talk it over and see." There was a pause, and Reverend. Burke suddenly exclaimed with a sigh of relief, as if he had been searching for something, "Ah! Here they are! I thought perhaps I had lost them!"

"What's that?" Stuart asked, peering through the darkness toward something his companion was holding in his hand.

"Black ore crystals—very rare specimens. If you have a match with you, I will show you."

Stuart could not help laughing. After all, he was still alive and safe after quite an experience of terror. "I'm afraid," he said, "that any matches I might have had would hardly work after the soaking I've had. I was in water up to my neck."

"I beg your pardon," Andrew Burke replied. He seemed somewhat embarrassed, but then as they were walking up the street to the house, he said gently, "You see, I was taking a geology walk this afternoon, which is how I came to explore the old Beury tunnel. I found these crystals and was putting them in my pocket when I heard your cry for help. I was kneeling on the floor of the tunnel and had my head near the sides of the wall at the time, or I doubt I would have heard you. So perhaps you won't think I'm simply a crank searching for specimens since this hunt led me to something better."

"It was a fortunate find for us," replied Stuart. "Eric and I will always be thankful for your search. I'm worried about him. Please come in, and I'll have one of the servants show you where you may make yourself at home for the night."

They hurried in, arriving just after the doctor and the miners. Then Stuart, after directing one of the servants to see to Reverend Burke, went to Eric. The doctor was examining and dressing his wound.

"He's had quite a hard blow, but nothing fatal. We'll pull him through. You'd better take off those wet clothes and take care of yourself. Thank God, you're alive, Stuart! I'm afraid this is just the beginning of trouble here. Unless I'm mistaken, what happened on the hill today is no coincidence. That rock didn't fall down the ladder hole by accident, and the engine house didn't burn without someone's help."

Stuart looked thoughtful. He was still in a miner's outfit, and if this occasion had not been so serious, the doctor might have been excused for smiling at his young friend's appearance. He was covered with greasy red iron-ore mud, having big streaks of it on his face and hands. But the gravity of the events and the apparent crisis ahead left little room for anything but a somber mood.

Stuart was standing over Eric. "Poor guy! This comes at a bad time for him."

"Yes, and for us too!" the doctor said sharply. "There's no telling what the men will do without Eric's influence to keep them quiet. And it will be weeks before he's up and around."

"I hadn't thought of that!" Stuart put his hand on Eric's forehead. At that moment Eric opened his eyes. He was conscious and began speaking, although feebly.

"Stuart, you saved my life. You've settled an old debt, and now we are even."

"Eric, we understand each other now, don't we?" Stuart spoke very directly, almost as a spouse would speak to his lifelong mate. "But we owe our lives to another man."

"How's that?" Eric was too weak to say more.

"I'll tell you when you are stronger. Please rest now."

Eric closed his eyes, and Stuart went to change his clothes. As he did he was struck with the conviction that his involvement in the present crisis of events had in part led to this evening's strange adventure.

Louise had gone somewhere to spend the evening with her friends, the Vasplaines. So Stuart, the doctor, and the new minister sat down to a late dinner by themselves, and it was while eating that Stuart learned the details of his rescue.

There was little more for Andrew Burke to tell. He was a stranger to the town, but in just two days of residing in Champion he had certainly made the most of his time. Seeing a miner on the path, he had inquired about the Beury tunnel just before entering it to search for crystals. The miner had volunteered the information regarding the connecting passageway with the lower level of the Davis mine. And Burke had not thought of it again until he heard Stuart's cry for help.

"Do you always carry a rope with you on your afternoon walks?" Stuart asked.

"No, I've not been in the habit of doing that, but it might just be a very useful idea in this mining country," Burke replied. "The rope was actually lying on the platform at the top of the last row of ladders, so I carried it with me, not knowing what I might need at the bottom. I guess the men had left it there when they went on strike. And I noticed their tools lying around in different places as I came through the drift."

The doctor looked at the new minister with strong approval. A man who could remember details like that was worth knowing. Rev. Andrew Burke was evidently on his way to establishing the doctor's friendship.

"But how did you happen to come after us?" Stuart asked, this time addressing the doctor.

"I was up at Rollins's place—you know, the pump man who was

53

hurt. His boy, the same one who came to my office the other day, ran in and said the engine house was on fire. And after what seemed like an eternity, we managed to pull out of him the fact that he had seen you and Eric go down the ladders a little while before. I rushed over to the shaft, but here's the real mystery of it to me. Not a soul was in sight. The engineer, firemen, and pump men were all gone. The ladders were blazing. There was no hope of descending on them. Some of the other men ran up from downtown. Then we remembered the Beury tunnel and ran toward it. You know, Stuart, it's more than a quarter of a mile from the shaft, but we made it in just a few minutes. I tripped on a rock and smashed a lot of valuable bottles in my case. You've cost me quite a lot, Stuart, beginning with the day you were born—you and Eric both. I don't know that stubbing my toe for that hotheaded young socialist and agitator is worth it. He's going to cause quite a bit of trouble in this world, and perhaps in the interest of humanity I should give him a little dose of something to finish him off."

Then Eric, in the room across the hall, stirred and groaned. The doctor heard him, dropped his napkin absentmindedly into his soup, and hurried in to see his "socialist" patient.

Before he came back, Stuart and Burke discussed the engine house fire. Something about it still seemed strange. Also, Stuart believed that the chunk of iron ore that fell on Eric was more than just a loose fragment from the side of the mine. The doctor was right about that. And the fact that no one was around when the fire broke out needed an explanation.

Once the doctor returned to the room, the three men continued to resolve these questions over dinner. But as they discussed them, they heard the footsteps of men marching up the road. The three rose as a group from the table, for the sound they heard was unmistakably menacing. Stuart walked directly into the hall and opened the large front door. The light of the porch lamp illuminated a crowd of at least two hundred men. Each one carried a stick or, more precisely, a club. The men were a formidable-looking mob, with their somber and stern faces lit by the electric lamp in the surrounding darkness of the night.

"Well, men," Stuart said clearly, "what do you want?"

The men crowded more closely to the porch. One of them, acting as spokesman, climbed onto the steps and said in a loud voice, "We want to see Eric."

"You can't see him. He's hurt and in no condition to see anyone!" shouted the doctor, who stood just behind Stuart in the doorway.

"Why do you want to see him?" Stuart asked calmly.

The spokesman appeared confused and didn't answer immediately. Then several in the crowd began shouting.

"There's been foul play!"

"We'll string up the men that did it!"

"Yeah! Hang 'em!"

"Let us see Eric! We want him with us tonight!"

"Men," Stuart said, raising his voice, "Gordon here can come in and see for you that Eric is unable to move. Come in, Gordon, and see," continued Stuart, speaking to the miner who was standing on the steps.

The miner, after a moment's hesitation, went into the house. The doctor followed him into the room at the right of the hall where Eric lay injured.

While they were gone, Stuart told the men how Eric got hurt. The men listened breathlessly to Stuart, and just as he finished, Gordon returned.

"Boys," he said as he stepped onto the porch, "Eric's out of it tonight. We'll take care of the cowards that did this."

"Yes! We will!" cried a dozen voices.

"Three cheers for Mr. Duncan!" one voice suddenly shouted. The men seemed to perceive from their own mining experiences that Stuart had stayed with Eric during the dangerous episode, although he had said very little about himself in relating the story.

The men heartily cheered three times, and for the first time in Stuart's life he felt that perhaps a day would come when these men would understand him. However, stepping from the doorway and pointing to where Andrew Burke was standing, he said, "Thank you, men. But if it hadn't been for Reverend Burke here, Eric would not be alive. We owe our lives to him."

"Who's he?" someone rudely asked.

"The new minister at St. John's. I know him," replied another.

"A minister? Well, three cheers for him anyway!" shouted another.

The men cheered again and then began to back away. Stuart was worried, and though already exhausted from his adventure earlier that evening, he could not help feeling that more tough work lay ahead before this night would be ended. He also believed it was a perfect opportunity to say a few words to the men while he was still in their good graces.

"Men, I would like to say something. I understand the troops are in town tonight. I hope you will all be law-abiding and—"

"Yeah, we've heard that till we're sick of it!" The voice was evidently that of a drunken man.

For the first time Stuart realized that the saloon was now becoming a factor in the problem. Before then, the men had stayed away from alcohol.

"Shut up!" exclaimed Gordon and a few others. "Give Mr. Duncan a fair hearing."

"I said," continued Stuart, "that I hope you will not become violent. I am talking to you as I know Eric would if he were here."

"But these troops have been brought in to take bread out of our mouths!"

"Yeah! That's the truth, and we'll take care of them as well!"

"This is not an order, just some friendly advice, you under-stand," Stuart said. Each minute he became more aware of the rest-lessness of the mob that had been deprived of their regular leader. "I advise you to go quietly to your homes. Tomorrow we'll inves-tigate the fire at the engine house and Eric's injury."

"What's the matter with tonight?" called out another man. The voice was calm and clear.

"Very well," replied Stuart energetically, hoping that any moment the restlessness of the men might be diverted in another direction. "It's my opinion that whoever burned the engine house overpowered the men there and has them hidden some-where right now. Do we have any men here from the Davis mine?"

The miners, familiar with each and every face in the Champion mines, answered in many places, "Not a man."

"Nobody has seen any Davis men since the shaft was burned?" Stuart asked.

"Mr. Duncan's hit on the answer! He's pretty bright."

"Now then, men, if I'm right about this, the men are hidden with the Davis crew. They can't be far away."

"We'll find 'em!" yelled more than one voice.

"Hold on! Wait a minute!" Stuart shouted as the men began to move again. "I want you to give me your word that if you find the men who did this, you will not attempt to punish them. They are guilty of breaking the law, so let's let the law deal with them. Thus far you have community support because of your good conduct, but the minute you resort to violence of any kind, public sympa-thy will vanish. Please give me your word that if you find these men, you will hand them over to the proper authorities."

At first there was silence, but then several voices responded, "We promise. Yes, we give our word."

Stuart was satisfied, although several men who were under the

57

influence of alcohol had not responded. The men walked from Stuart's lawn, while he and Andrew Burke watched a large part of the mob head directly up the hill toward the smoldering remains of the engine house. The other men trudged off into town.

"There is going to be trouble in this town tonight," the doctor said. He went in to see Eric again. Stuart and the minister stayed in the hall. As they talked, Stuart was expressing his concerns about the mob of men when his telephone rang.

He answered the phone and talked for a moment. Then turning to Reverend Burke, he said, "Are you able to go somewhere this evening?"

"Yes, I've got a bit of a limp from tonight, and I do not look very presentable, but I feel okay to go somewhere."

Stuart went to the hall closet and got an overcoat for Reverend Burke. As he put on his own coat, he said, "I've just been given a message from the Iron Cliffs Company that the miners are gathering in the town square, becoming a huge mob. I was told I'd better get down there and use my influence to prevent a riot."

"Are you able to do that tonight?" questioned Reverend Burke.

"Yes, I guess so. Like you, I'm sore and limping, but have no broken bones. I feel it's my duty to go. Besides, the doctor will stay here and watch Eric."

"Oh, he will, will he!" the doctor said as he came from the room behind Stuart. "You need to be watched as much as Eric. Take off that overcoat, and go upstairs to bed!"

"Now, Doctor," Stuart replied with a sad smile, "I don't like to say I won't, but I will this time. I feel that I should go to the square. I'm fearful of the bad things that may happen tonight, but at least Reverend Burke and I will be there to protest."

"All right, go on—both of you! But when you get your heads broken, don't send for me to glue the pieces together again."

The doctor went back to Eric, Stuart ordered the servants to bring his horse and buggy around, and then he and Reverend Burke quickly descended the stairs and drove hurriedly away.

As they sped down the hill, they passed several groups of miners almost rhythmically marching along the road at a rapid pace. When Stuart and the reverend reached the square, there was such a large crowd overflowing into the streets that Stuart drove into a nearby alley and hitched his horse near the church at the rear. They then entered the square in the area next to the church and the railroad station platform.

The miners were not in the habit of assembling at night, since all of their meetings up to that point had been at noon. The present gathering was a new development of the strike. As Stuart and the minister crowded in with the others at the corner near the church, both of them realized the town had all the makings of a very serious problem being compressed into that spot—its commercial and social center.

In the first place there was an unusually large number of drunken men in the mob, and it was growing noisier every minute. The stage was crowded with miners. Two of them were trying to speak at the same time at opposite ends of the stage, and they seemed to be doubling the confusion. The mob moved restlessly around the stage area, which was lit by an electric hanging lamp that made the square nearly as bright as daytime.

On a side track of the railroad, skirting one side of the square, stood the coaches that had brought in the troops that afternoon and that were now their quarters. There were two companies, and for some reason they had been ordered to remain in Champion all night. Every mention of the troops seemed to excite the miners to anger, and each speaker on the stage referred to them often and pointed toward their train. A lot had happened that day—enough to stir up even the normally sluggish, solemn men of the North. Eric's injury, which upset many of the men, was a cause for rejoicing by another large and rowdy faction. They were glad to have his leadership displaced by more radical, although less capable men.

Stuart couldn't help thinking, *If only Eric were here!* For the first time he realized the great power Eric possessed. It was no small feat of leadership to hold this rough-and-tumble sea of uneducated men in check. Yet there was no one to take Eric's place.

Stuart had no definite plan to pursue in coming down to the square. When the miners saw him, they spoke respectfully and asked about Eric. Finally, he and Reverend Burke found themselves crowded onto the church steps, which were covered with men.

It was now about eight-thirty, and although they were tired from the day's events, the scene caused the two men to look at the faces below them with a certain level of excitement that grew with each passing second. The noise and confusion were increasing, and a fight of some kind was already in progress near the stage. Bodies seemed to sway back and forth from the press of the crowd. The police force of Champion was small in any event, but was powerless to manage a crowd of such magnitude. It might as well have been comprised of little children.

Suddenly, rising above all the other sounds in the square was that of a drumbeat. It was not simply the feeble rattle of sticks, but a determined, vigorous, and muscular onslaught of a bass drum by a strong right arm. Then around the corner by the Iron Cliffs Company's office came a squad of men and women, not more than a dozen in all, bearing a flag and shouting as they came:

> *Our boat is sailing o'er life's sea, to a land beyond the blue,*
> *We're going to the promised land 'long with the chosen few;*
> *Aboard the boat there still is room for many, many more,*
> *So come aboard and with us go to yonder happy shore.*
> *Our boat is laden down with wealth, with pleasures rich*
> *and rare:*

There's naught like them upon the earth, and we all may
have a share.
Just leave behind all worldly dross and come to God's own store,
Receive your gifts and with them cross to yonder happy shore.

The Salvation Army marched straight across the street, singing the hymn to the tune of "O' a' the airts the winds can blaw," and as they reached the side of the square, a strange thing happened.

The miners on that side opened up a passage for the little squad so that it could pass into the square. Then as if acting on that initial impulse, the miners began to move back on both sides, while the Salvation Army kept advancing. They sang and marched in what seemed almost like a triumphal procession directly through the center of the square and up to the church steps. The huge crowd seemed to part like magic, so the small group marched down its newly formed "avenue," beating its drum. The leader was a young woman whose pale face possessed a prematurely aged look, yet there was not a hint of self-consciousness to be seen upon it. She marched proudly at the front as if she were a queen being followed by the handpicked archangels of the heavenly hosts. Wafting over the shrill treble and the deep bass of the others, her voice was as sweet as any voice Stuart had ever heard. He wondered how such a voice had been hidden in Champion without his ever hearing it. She sang as if the words were sacred to her heart:

Just leave behind all worldly dross and come to God's own store,
Receive your gifts and with them cross to yonder happy shore.

The band stopped near the foot of the church steps where the crowd was closely packed together. It seemed to be the perfect place for testimony and appeal, and the miners, at least for now, appeared to yield to the influence of this new attraction. Stuart said to himself,

"Perhaps Eric will not be needed, after all." This new scene had his intense interest, and he temporarily forgot all about Burke and the strike and his relation to it. The woman then raised her hand as a signal for the drum to cease, and then made another signal for the little company to kneel. She knelt on one of the bottom steps, just below Stuart, nearly drowned by the sea of men kneeling around her. She then offered up a prayer, the memory of which would linger in Stuart's heart the rest of his life.

4

a change in Stuart

Lord Jesus," the pale face in the Salvation Army bonnet was raised, seemingly unaware of all the people in that great multitude, "our hearts are longing tonight for lost souls, who have wandered far away from home. And we know You are sorrowing over them even now because You are the Good Shepherd. O Lord Jesus, we want You to come down here tonight and lead some of these sheep into the fold. Many of them are so bruised and torn by sin that they will have to be carried. But, O Lamb of God who takes away the sin of the world, we know You are strong and can carry them in the arms of infinite love over rough places, the chasms of Satan, and through the raging torrents of death. May the cross of Calvary be stretched out like great saving arms tonight! Oh, may the sweet forgiveness of sin touch these human hearts right now!

"O Son of Mary, our hearts are bleeding and we are deathly weary of the long-delayed coming of the miracle of redemption in the souls of these men. Oh, bless us with the blood of the dying Savior! Raise us to new life with Him who defied hell and death in that battle of two against one! Jesus, I want You to come here tonight. These men—these women—how precious they are! Who knows what their fate would be if they were called from this world tonight? Their dear mothers, Lord Jesus . . . Some of these strong young men have mothers praying for them. Oh, I can only imagine the terror of the judgment for those who reject the Savior!

"We are in great need of Your power here and now. Open our eyes tonight to see Your horses and chariots of fire surrounding us, just as You did for the young man of old. Save with Your blood that was shed for all. Come now, Lord Jesus. We have followed. Make good Your promise. Yes, we want some souls. We are hungry for some to cry out, 'Saved! Saved!' We want to march triumphantly into the judgment. We want to sing hallelujah before the Great White Throne with some of these poor lost sinners here standing by our side and joining in the chorus with us. Oh, wash their sins away in the precious blood! Save them, save them, Lord Jesus!"

It was not so much the words of the prayer as it was the intense humility and self-forgetful spirit that impressed Stuart as never before in his life. He was not a Christian in the sense that he had ever confessed Christ or joined a church. Yet he had a reverent nature, and he had always lived by a code of morality that seemed sufficient for him. He was too well educated, or so he thought, to be moved by anything purely emotional or as bold as the Salvation Army with its drums and shouting. But somehow, this was different. What swept over him from this prayer were the self-forgetfulness, the self-surrender, and the agonizing for souls to be saved, all coming from this slight womanly form who knelt there. Never in all of his experience—never in all his visiting of great cathedrals or listening to chanted services—had he felt closer to the true knowledge of who God is and His great compelling love for sinful men.

All this took very little time, and he had no intention of acting in any way on his feelings. But while the woman was still on her knees, something happened that ultimately deepened his conviction and changed the future course of events among the miners themselves.

The crowd was so large that only a very few could see or hear what was going on around the little band at the foot of the church steps. At least up to that time, the Salvation Army in Champion had great influence over the miners. It was still true, but it was also true tonight that "the demon of drink" was running rampant, which always brings an unsettling and unpredictable factor to any given situation. The men closest to the small band were being pushed by those farther out who wanted to see and hear what was going on. To prevent being crushed into the little company, the miners had been silently exerting their great strength to keep the mob back during the entire prayer.

Before the kneeling woman could stand, however, a group of drunken men burst through the circle that had formed around her. One of them kicked the drum, sending his heavy boot right through it, while another man drunkenly staggered toward the woman, raising his fist and cursing. Stuart, as he saw the man's face, thought that perhaps the rum-crazed man imagined the kneeling woman to be his own wife, who had more than once begged him on her knees to spare her and her children.

It all happened in a flash, and Stuart dealt the man a blow with his fist that knocked him swearing against a man behind him. Before anyone else could raise his arm again to strike a blow, the miners had seized every one of the assailants who were attacking the Salvation Army, and a roar went up from the entire mob of excited and angry men. The influence of the Army was still so strong in the vast majority that they deeply resented any indignity offered its little band of officers.

"Duck 'em in the fountain!" yelled someone with more than a touch of grim humor.

The "fountain" was a huge cast-iron basin in the center of the square, which for several years had been used as a watering trough. It had about four feet of water in it that was pumped there from the mines.

The idea was perfectly suited to the coarse, rough spirit of the crowd. Struggling in the clutches of the mob's brawny hands, the offenders were dragged to the basin and thrown into it. Yet as fast as they tramped out, dripping and cursing, they were thrown in again. A huge roar of laughter and shouting rose from the mob, while in the midst of it all the Army marched out of the square, singing:

> Come, sinners, to the Savior now;
> He wore the thorn-crown on His brow;
> He shed His blood that you might be
> Redeemed to all eternity.
> No more delay, for pardon cry;
> Jesus your Savior is passing by.

The leader of the Army had the same fearless look on her face. No one could say that she was disappointed or disheartened by the seeming lack of answer to her prayer or by the wild confusion all about her. The small group stopped in the street, while another group gathered around them to listen to testimonies, prayers, and songs.

Stuart and the minister hesitated where they were for a moment, not knowing what to do next. Suddenly, part of the crowd farthest away near the railroad tracks began running as a group toward a smaller crowd descending the hill from the Davis mine.

"I believe they must have caught the men who did the burning!" Stuart cried to Burke. The two forced their way through the crowd toward the hill and were met there by the same mob that had earlier come to the house demanding to see Eric.

The incoming group marched into the square, and one of them went directly to the stage to share the news. They had found the engineer, fireman, and pump men about a mile up the hill, locked in an old dry room that belonged to a recently abandoned mine. They were securely tied, but uninjured. There was no trace of the men who had locked them up with the obvious intent of setting the engine house on fire and getting rid of Eric and Stuart—the two men who would likely insist on law and order as long as they had influence with the miners. Yet, to the credit of thousands of miners in all the hills around Champion, the attempt was regarded by the vast majority as a cowardly and murderous act, a disgrace to hardworking men, and a setback to the cause. There was especially great anger expressed against the attempt to kill or injure Eric by throwing that massive chunk of ore down the ladder hole. It had been no accident according to one of the men who had been overpowered at the mouth of the shaft and had been one of the unwilling witnesses to the outrage.

The appearance of the Davis men, and the relating of their story, had a sobering effect on the crowd, causing it to disperse. The troops were forgotten for a while. Anyway, the new miners that the owners from the upper hills had sent would not arrive in Champion until tomorrow. Several groups of miners then began walking toward their homes, and Stuart saw that the danger for the evening was passed. The Salvation Army had marched off to its hall, and a large crowd had followed it. As the square began to rapidly clear, and Stuart realized that the night's stress had indeed ended, he felt completely exhausted.

"Will you stay at my house tonight, Reverend Burke?" he asked as the two walked from the square to where the horse was still tied.

"No, Mr. Duncan. I believe I will remain down here, since I'm now so close to my hotel room, but thanks anyway. This has certainly been quite a day for you. I hope you will be none the worse for it. The danger from the men seems over for tonight."

"Yes, I think so. I'm sorry you're not going with me. And you're right—this has been quite a day. I'll never forget my indebtedness to you. I'm sure we'll know each other better as a result of today's events, and I need to know as many good men as possible these days."

"I'm at your service, Mr. Duncan. Good night!"

"Good night." Stuart firmly shook hands and drove up the street, again feeling a tingling sensation from the pressure of Burke's grasp. Andrew Burke's handshake spoke nearly as much as some orators' speeches.

Stuart was so tired and in need of rest when he got home that he quickly went to his room, after having checked on Eric. He was assured that Eric would be fine throughout the night and would be watched by the nurse that the doctor had sent.

He slept hard, but wakened early and could not go to sleep again. He dreamed of his experience in the mine and awoke at the point where he heard Burke's voice. He went over the whole episode again, then was irresistibly drawn in thought to the town square, and saw himself again standing on the church steps just above the kneeling woman who had prayed. He found himself repeating the words of the prayer, and to his surprise, he could remember almost every sentence. Then he began to analyze the feelings that the prayer had provoked. He was unable to criticize anything in the prayer, and with no apparent reason, he began asking if the saving of the men should not be as much his business as that of the Salvation Army. He began to dwell on the word *saved* as it was used so often in the prayer. Then, as a logical step that he did not attempt to argue about as he might have done before, he was confronted with his own condition. And although he tried to avoid answering the questions, they persisted in being asked, "Am I saved? What is Jesus to me?"

The entire matter was foreign to his moral code. Besides, how could someone in his current condition, with all the labor trouble confronting him, bother with religious questions? Nevertheless, he was forced to return to the simple questions, "Am I saved? What is Jesus to me?" Throughout the strange debate going on inside him, he felt he was being irresistibly driven to the point where he must answer or decide the matter of his personal salvation.

He dressed, and in growing excitement he walked the room in the twilight. How are men converted? Was Saul of Tarsus expecting to be met by the vision on the road to Damascus? Wasn't it as sudden and astonishing to him as a lightning bolt out of a cloudless evening? Does the Lord have any certain limitations in His way of reaching men's souls or on the time He chooses? Stuart tried again and again to stop the persistent questions that rose repeatedly to his lips, but to no avail.

He thought, *I'll go downstairs and see about Eric.* But each time he faced the door, he turned again and paced back to the windows toward the front of the house. Gradually, as the daylight grew brighter outside in the world, an inward light grew brighter in Stuart's soul. He felt it grow and was awed by its strange revealing power. He saw himself as a child of God, with opportunities, powers, and values. Prior to that he had selfishly used these things, but now he saw an illuminated, radiant cross shining through it all.

"What was Jesus to him?" The question grew with meaning. Why was the Jesus of history Someone to be respected? Of what value and meaning was the cross unless it became a personal redemption? The sunrise of the outer world was reddening the pines on the hills. In a little while the sun would be looking out over the ranges and a new day would be born. But a new man was being born in the room of the Champion iron mine owner. The Sun of Righteousness was rising in him, and soon it would be daylight.

Stuart trembled. He was alone. No one had spoken to him of salvation or of Christianity. But the divine presence had come at an unexpected moment—at what might have seemed a most inopportune time. But his whole being was in the hand of a Power that he dared not resist. He nearly feared to breathe, lest he drive the heavenly presence away. He sat down and with his head bowed waited, it seemed to him, for something more to happen. And then he seemed to hear a voice say, *My son, give Me your heart.* He clasped his hands together and replied, "God, be merciful to me a sinner!" and with the words a flood of light poured in. He at once knelt down—an unusual thing for him. But it seemed as necessary as breathing, and filled him with joy and with love.

He could not tell how long he had been in that deep communion with his Savior, so newly found. It must have been some time, for he was startled by one of the servants knocking at the door to announce breakfast. He went downstairs, and the first person he met in the hallway was Louise. Stuart had entered a new world that he would better come to know, and his heart went out to his sister this morning with a new tenderness. She put her arm around his neck as he stooped to kiss her.

"What a dreadful time you must have had, Stuart! It's a wonderful blessing you weren't killed in that awful mine. The doctor has been telling me all about it."

"Yes, I feel as if my life has been spared for some great reason," Stuart replied. "How is Eric this morning?" He put his arm around Louise and moved with her toward the door of Eric's nearby room. Louise slipped away from him and answered, "Oh, he's getting better. I don't want to see him. Don't forget to come to breakfast, Stuart."

She crossed the hall into the dining room and Stuart went to see Eric, who still lay in the downstairs bedroom—one of the features of the house that remained since Ross Duncan had first designed and built it.

The doctor was standing near the bed. He had come early that morning to attend to the wound. Eric was resting comfortably, but lay there looking very pale and almost stern. Stuart felt an added tenderness for the man who had been his friend during their hour of danger. And somehow his experience earlier this morning had deepened and enlarged all his feelings of friendship and love.

He knelt down by the bed and smiled as Eric turned his dark eyes toward him. "What sort of night did you have, dear friend?" he asked as he laid his hand in Eric's.

"Oh, I rested well. I'm able to get up this morning, but the doctor here won't let me move."

"You can get up if you want to," replied Dr. Saxon gruffly. "And Stuart, please order my horse to be brought around so I can get to the undertaker's in time to make arrangements with him for Eric's funeral. Do you want the hearse with the black plumes all around the top, or the other one with the weeping urn arrangement in the middle?"

"Nonsense! I'm not as bad off as that!" replied Eric with a feeble attempt at a smile.

"You will be if you get out of that bed before two weeks," replied the doctor as he gathered up his things to go. "Besides, you couldn't get up by yourself if you tried. Stuart, I'm leaving him in your care. The nurse will be able to attend to him. She has my complete instructions." And with a word or two more the doctor went out of the house, jumped in his carriage, and raced down the hill.

Stuart remained a few minutes with Eric and then went to breakfast. There was a good deal to talk over with Louise, and she asked many questions about the "accident." Stuart answered, feeling all the time that everybody around him had changed since that Light had dawned upon him. Even Louise could see and feel a difference, although she could not tell what it was. Finally, she abruptly stopped asking her questions about the mines and said, "What's the matter with you, Stuart? What has happened? Are you sick from the effects of your exposure to the cold water yesterday?"

Stuart looked across the table at her and it was several moments before he replied. Then he said, "I'll tell you, Louise, when we have more time alone. I want time to think now. No, I am not sick. In fact, I feel better than I have in a long time."

Louise looked surprised, but asked nothing more, and went on to tell about the gathering at the Vasplaines' the prior evening. Stuart listened thoughtfully, now and then asking a question. Louise returned to the subject of the miners. "Now that troops have been ordered here, I suppose the strike will end, won't it?"

"I don't know. Maybe it has just begun."

"But don't you intend to hire new men? All the mines in the lower hills are bringing in new men today. It's an outrage for the men to prevent others from working!"

"There will be trouble, I'm afraid, before the day is over," Stuart replied. He was facing a very serious problem, and he found his heart crying out for wisdom to the divine Source he was beginning to know.

"Well, I don't understand you, Stuart. If Father were alive, he would have a thousand men here in Champion ready to go to work this morning instead of waiting for the other men to accept the terms he had offered, only to have them foolishly rejected. If they won't work on their own terms, which you say you offered them, how can they blame you if you get new men in and protect them with troops? If I were a man, I would teach those men a lesson! And look at the way they've treated you and Eric. They—"

Louise looked prettier than ever as she stamped her foot beneath the table. Stuart remained silent and somber. Just then the telephone rang, so he went to answer it. After a few moments he returned to tell Louise he would have to go down to the Iron Cliffs office. Word had been sent up that he was needed.

"Aunt Royal is coming in on the noon train, Stuart. You remember? Should I drive down to get her?"

"Yes, Louise. I'm not sure how much time this morning's business will take. Please see to her for me." Stuart leaned over Louise as she sat at the table and kissed her again.

"Stuart, do use some common sense about this strike business. Hire new men. What can you do if all the other owners start up again?"

"I'll do the right and best thing," replied Stuart gently as he went into Eric's room for a minute.

"I'm sorry to leave you, Eric," he said affectionately.

Eric groaned. "Of all the times in my life to be lying here! Stuart, I must get up and go with you. The men . . ."

Eric tried to raise himself up, but fell back with a cry of pain. The sweat beaded up on his forehead in large drops, then he clenched his fists and his teeth in a bit of a rage that was not only terrible to see but pitiful as well.

As Stuart stood by Eric, he felt great compassion in his heart for him. "Eric, you will have to be patient. After all, many of the men have not disregarded the law during this strike. With the exception of the men who burned the engine house, I believe most of the miners are determined to be law-abiding."

"Not if they're going to be drinking," Eric replied. He winced from the pain. "They are devils when they drink. Curse the saloons! They'll be the ruin of our cause yet. Tell me, Stuart, that you'll do all you can to keep the men under control. The troops are coming in today, and the new workers. O Lord, if only I were with my men today, I believe I could control them!"

"Yes, Eric, I'll do my best. After all, aren't we in the hands of Someone who knows the end from the beginning?"

Eric stared at Stuart in astonishment. Stuart continued as he leaned over the bed, "Eric, the Light has shone upon me. God has spoken to me, and I am a Christian. It has all happened to me very suddenly."

Eric was too bewildered to understand all Stuart meant by his confession, but he feebly returned Stuart's handshake. Then Stuart simply added, "I'll tell you more when I get back." After a pause he continued, "God bless you, Eric! And God help us to solve this conflict with His wisdom, for ours is weak and foolish."

Eric shut his eyes as silent tears began running from his closed eyelids across his pale cheeks. Then Stuart left his side.

He hurried into town and drove first to Eric's cottage, which was on a side street three blocks from the square. Eric's father and mother were dead, and he was not married. He lived with his grandmother and two cousins, young boys who expected to become miners in due time. Eric's home life was strange, and had certainly influenced his life and shaped it to what it was today. Stuart left word with Eric's grandmother that Eric would be staying with him for a while, and then drove back into the square and went into his office.

It was his father's old office, but ever since Ross Duncan's death it had become a sort of headquarters for several mine owners who had railroad interests in Champion and mining property in other ranges of the hills. Three or four of the men greeted Stuart as he came in, but immediately began to argue with him about his stance regarding the strike and his probable influence on the outcome of it.

"Now, Duncan," one of the men said before pausing. He was a large man who wore a heavy watch chain and looked important, but was somewhat overdressed. "It is necessary for us all to work together in this matter. Things have now come to the point where we must either run our own businesses or have them run for us by a lot of wild, ignorant fanatics controlled by those Salvation Army cranks and other fools of that sort."

It was all Stuart could do to keep from striking the man in the mouth as he spoke of the Salvation Army. His imagination and his memory caused his eyes to look past the big man and through the window to the scenes of the previous evening. All he could see was that delicate face in the Army bonnet, and that kneeling woman in the midst of that mob. And all he could hear was that prayer from that sweet, clear, and refined voice. Yet the fact that Stuart calmly listened until the man finished speaking was good evidence of the genuineness of his new manhood. He waited and then quietly said, "I don't think of the Salvation Army as you do, Mr. Wyman. My closest friend, Eric Vassall, is a member of it. And, in fact, I believe we owe the lack of lawlessness during this strike to the religious influence exerted by the Army."

Stuart's reply surprised all the other men. The big man turned red and was about to say something when one of the others spoke up. "That aside, Mr. Duncan, we still don't see your reason for refusing to hire new men and start up again. Your refusal to do so just encourages the strikers."

"I believe they ought to have the wages they're demanding," Stuart calmly replied.

"Well, we don't!" the first speaker viciously exclaimed. "I'll see every striker starve before I'll grant anything like the terms they want. The current price of ore will never allow it."

"But," said another man, speaking to Stuart, who remained standing in the middle of the room, "the Cleveland men are determined to put new men to work today. The first group will arrive on the noon train, and troops are coming with them. The two companies of troops that were here last night went on down to the lower range of hills early this morning. We have the game won if we will only work together. Duncan, you are the largest mine owner here. A great deal depends on your actions."

Stuart seemed to be pondering what the man had said, while the men anxiously stared at him. Finally, he looked straight at them, as his face lit up. "I've given the men my word that I would take them back on their terms. Yet they have refused to come back unless all the other owners agree to the same terms. I still think that I am right in this matter, and that the rest of you ought to grant their demands. If I am to remain true to my own convictions, I could never do otherwise. Besides, my current refusal to hire new men is certainly not adding to the danger of the situation here in Champion. Gentlemen—" Stuart paused for a moment, then firmly continued, "I cannot see my way clear to hire the men at wages lower than two dollars a day. I do not agree with the statement that the price of ore does not warrant the increase in wages, for I firmly believe it does. The plain fact of the matter is that the work is so dangerous and difficult that two dollars a day is very little for their labor. There isn't one of us here or in Cleveland who would do the work these men do for twenty dollars a day! I just don't see it the way you do. I will do my best to prevent trouble, but if my men come back at any time during the strike, I will reopen the mines and pay two dollars a day for anyone who works underground."

The men looked at Stuart with increasing astonishment. There was total silence in the office, which was broken by the big man who had spoken first. He proclaimed, "Well, that beats me! I never expected to hear the son of Ross Duncan make a socialist labor speech! You ought to join their party, sir!"

The tone of the man's remark was so offensive to Stuart that he became pale and started to tremble, but he controlled his emotions and turned to the other men. The men talked excitedly for another half hour, while the big man sulked and smoked a bad cigar in the corner. Stuart realized he was not and could not be understood. Yet he felt he could not give his best reasons for his position to these men. They lay too deeply at the foundation of his newly found life to be explained to men whose spiritual natures were buried under a mere financial existence.

When he was convinced that all the talk in the world would not satisfy the other men, Stuart left. He felt the need for someone who could relate and respond to his life, for these men caused him to feel choked and poisoned. He could not think of words less strong to describe his feelings as he realized the firm grasp the love of money had on the business world. All the while his heart cried out, "God, help me! I want to do the right thing, and will do it as fast as You light the way." He examined his stance regarding the strike thus far in the new light of his Christian discipleship, but heard no accusing voice in his heart over what he believed to be just. As he went out to the street he was at peace, at least as far as that was concerned.

Walking down the street, thinking it all over, Stuart had a strong desire to talk with someone he could trust—someone who could sympathize with him. He immediately thought of the new minister. "I ought to go and see about him anyway." He picked up his pace while crossing the street, entered the square, and took a diagonal path to the hotel where Burke was staying.

He saw Andrew Burke walking through the hotel lobby with a large box. When Burke saw Stuart, he exclaimed, "Come here! Come here, Mr. Duncan! I've got some beauties here. I want you to see them."

Stuart followed him up one flight of stairs, and they entered a large room in the corner of the hotel. Andrew Burke set down his burden, firmly shook hands with Stuart, and opened his box. Stuart looked on wonderingly.

It was a box full of potted plants—most of them young roses. As fast as Burke took them out of the box, he arranged them on a shelf by the window.

"There's a Nyphetis, one of the most delicate roses going. And here is my Keizerine, a new variety just out this year. This Catherine Mermet is a beauty, yet very hard to get a bloom in this climate, I fear. The Safrano is better. And just look at this one! I raised this Meteor myself and had six magnificent blooms from it last winter! You see, Mr. Duncan, my wife was away visiting relatives back East when the call came for me to come here, and I try to amuse myself until she arrives with more roses. These are my pets. Let me show you more of my friends I've gotten since I've been here."

Rev. Andrew Burke brought out a tray from another room and set it down on the table near Stuart. Then he noticed the look on Stuart's face, and his whole demeanor made a swift and remarkable change. He suddenly looked and spoke like the strong and deep man that he really was, in spite of his pet roses.

"Mr. Duncan, you did not come here to talk botany with me, did you?"

"To tell the truth, I did not, Reverend Burke."

"What is it?" asked Andrew Burke, leaning forward and putting a hand on Stuart's arm.

It was a simple question and simply put. But it revealed such a genuinely strong desire to really know and understand Stuart that before he realized it, Stuart was relating his experience of earlier that morning. The tea-rose aroma from the plants in the window and on the table filled the room, and Andrew Burke listened with caring eyes and an occasional deep breath. "Thank God! Thank God!" he said as Stuart continued. When Stuart finally paused, Burke said, "Could we have a little prayer of thanksgiving over this—right here where we sit?"

"Yes, yes," replied Stuart gladly.

Before Andrew Burke was through with his prayer, Stuart was sobbing. It was the first real dose of Christian understanding he had ever known. It was wonderful to him to think that he was linked in mutual knowledge and understanding with every other Christian disciple. And over the next few minutes of sharing he experienced one of the most precious and sweetest joys of his life.

Soon Stuart found himself discussing the strike and its problems with Burke. It did not seem shocking to Stuart to be doing so, for after all, it was a part of his life. And shouldn't all of his life ahead be lived to the glory of God?

He was relieved to hear Burke agree with his decision regarding the miners' wages. "My sympathies are with the workmen, Mr. Duncan. In fact, I was born on a farm and raised in a factory. I'll tell you about it sometime."

"I'm going to make a request," Stuart said with a smile. "Do you think a man who saves another man's life ought to continue to call him 'Mister'?"

"What would you like for me to call you?"

"How about 'Stuart'? That's not hard to pronounce, is it?"

"No harder than 'Andrew.'"

"It's a deal then. No more 'Misters.'"

"Yes, but this is awfully sudden, young man!" Andrew Burke replied, rising from his chair and walking closer to Stuart. "Besides, I'm ten years your senior and should be giving you advice. But—yes, it's a deal."

The two men shook hands again after reaching their simple understanding. It was the Christian fellowship they shared that was making their fast friendship possible. If not for this common bond, they would probably have "mistered" each other to a gray old age, even if they had saved each other's life every day.

Events outside continued to speed along, and Stuart could not help feeling anxious over the noon train bringing in new men and additional troops. The miners were already gathering in the square and the two men, looking from the hotel window, could sense the level of excitement growing among the miners. This time, however, they were gathering near the train station rather than by the stage.

"I'm going down there, and if there is even a hint of trouble, I'll do everything in my power to prevent violence," Stuart said.

"I'll go with you," replied Andrew Burke.

The two of them stood close by the station platform as the noon train arrived. They witnessed the entire scene—something that no one there would ever forget.

The train pulled in slowly as the miners watched in somber silence. The first two coaches were filled with troops. The rest of the cars, six in all, contained the new workers.

No one knew until much later exactly how the events of that day had been planned and executed, but before the engineer or fireman could offer any resistance, or even think about doing so, they were pulled down from the cab of the engine. And in an instant the engine and tender were uncoupled from the coaches, and two miners who knew how to run an engine drove it forward, diverting it from the main track onto one near the ore chutes.

Meanwhile the miners at the rear of the train began calling out to the new workers in the coaches to get out and present themselves. "We want to see the brave men who've come to take bread out of our mouths! Show yourselves! Come out and get a taste of our clubs!"

While this was happening, an officer with the troops, seeing what had happened to the engine, promptly ordered his men out of the coaches. They then blocked the track beside the rear coaches to defend the men still on the train. The commanding officer was a handsome young man who seemed cool and determined. As the troops took their position, the crowd moved back somewhat, leaving a space of perhaps twenty feet between the troops and the crowd.

It was a critical moment that needed only one act of violence to precipitate a crisis—an act that would soon follow. As the officer turned to give a command, a drunken man threw a chunk of ore with murderous strength directly into his face. The officer fell to the ground with his blood spattering the uniform of the man next to him.

Stuart, still standing on the station platform, tried to make himself heard. However, the officer next in command stepped out, and in a voice that rose above the roar of even the savage mob, he shouted, "Make ready!" Before he could add, "Aim" and "Fire," a woman suddenly seemed to throw herself from the mob, and then ran directly in front of the guns leveled at the miners. She stood there alone in the narrow space between the troops and the men. Stuart recognized her as the Salvation Army leader he had seen the night before. Her face was pale, but she was calm and did not give the appearance that she felt she was doing anything out of the ordinary. Yet there she stood with the muzzles of those guns nearly touching her.

5

the standoff

The woman stood face-to-face with the soldiers for a moment. Then, breaking the deadly silence that was nearly as terrifying as the roar of the mob just a few seconds before, she turned and spoke.

"My brothers, in the name of God and His dear Son, our Savior, remember who you are, and if you value heaven, do no wrong today."

The miners listened, and the silence was unbroken. It was one of those times that test men, either showing them to be equal to or lacking in an emergency. And Stuart in that brief moment grew in strength and experience. Before Andrew or anyone else moved, Stuart had walked to the open space by the woman. Now the guns were leveled at them both, with the barrels actually touching them. The moment he stepped next to her in the space between the troops and the miners, the woman turned and knelt at the side of the injured officer. Stuart was consciously aware that the men were now carrying the injured man from their ranks and that the woman

82

was following, yet he seemed to be feeling rather than actually seeing it happen.

"Men," he said, praying in his heart for wisdom to say just the right words, "listen to me a moment! Every man who strikes an unlawful blow here today strikes against the cause of labor. If you want to set it back, destroying what is best for you, now is your opportunity. Yet you would have to be madmen to do that. In God's name, in the name of the law, and in your own best interests, I beg you to use reason. For the sake of Eric, who loves you if anyone ever did, let these men go their way, and accept the outcome as law-abiding and God-fearing men!"

There was a stir throughout the crowd while Stuart spoke. Then the silence was broken by shouts here and there from men who had helped Eric to organize the union.

"He's right! Mr. Duncan is telling the truth."

"Let's maintain law and order, or we'll be fools!"

"Yeah! Well, we're fools already."

"We must convince these new men to go back home!"

This last idea was suddenly shared by many, so the mob swarmed around the coaches containing the new men. Thus far, the men had stayed inside the train, but the windows were populated with heads trying to see what was happening.

The troops lowered their guns but remained on guard, and Stuart felt that the immediate danger of violence had ended. However, any number of opportunities remained for an outbreak.

The scene near the train now seemed extremely sad and pathetic in nature. Yet with it all there was still the element of danger that the fickle wild beast of the mob might stir once again.

"Now, boys," pleaded an older miner, who was standing close by one of the coaches, "you don't want to take bread out of our mouths here, do you? Come on now! Tell us you'll go back and leave us alone to fight it out with the bosses. We'll win if you'll leave us alone."

Another miner chimed in eagerly, "We all agree! The owners are losing money every day now. Give us a chance. Anyway, what have we done to you that you would come here to take our wages?"

"We have families too!" replied a gruff voice from one of the train windows. "There's been no work for more than a month for us, and our wives are at home with crying babies. What are we supposed to do?"

It was a difficult question to answer. No one even tried. Yet hundreds of voices were still beseeching the new miners to return home, leaving the owners to deal with their old workers.

Finally, a middle-aged miner, who was second only to Eric in influence in Champion and who had helped to organize the union, moved forward to speak. He climbed atop one of the railroad switching blocks, while the men anxiously awaited his words.

"Tell you what we'll do. We union members will pay the return fares of everyone here, plus a little something extra, if you'll go back home on the next train."

A hundred voices of Champion miners agreed, yelling, "Yes, we will!" The union, which numbered almost five thousand men, was in a position to do just that. In its desperate fight with the owners the union could better afford to squeeze every possible cent from its members than to give in to the influx of new workers. If the mines were to reopen now, the opportunity to bring the owners to terms would be gone forever. Besides, as public opinion within the town continued to grow and other workers began to side with the miners, there was no telling what could happen.

The miners were becoming quite frantic in their appeals to the new workers. They climbed onto the station platform and squeezed into the coaches to plead their case. It was a very strange scene, seeing the huge swarm of rough-and-tumble men begging a group of their peers to refrain from exercising their natural desire to provide for their own wives and children. The curse placed on Adam and Eve seemed doubled because in that situation the curse of work itself had become the object of the dispute between the two groups.

Some four hundred or more of the nearly five hundred new workers agreed to return home as long as the union would follow through on its monetary promises. It was difficult to tell whether their decision was made because of their sympathy with the other miners or because of the presence of a thousand men with clubs in hand.

As they stepped from the train, they were greeted with a tremendous burst of cheers and shouts. The few remaining men, who for one reason or another had refused to go back home, were greeted with hisses, jeers, threats, and verbal abuse—but no physical violence. The local miners were jubilant over the result of their appeal, but continued to ridicule the handful of men still resisting them.

"Leave 'em alone, boys! What can the owners do with such a sorry lot anyway?"

"Yeah, let 'em go! They don't have enough sense to get away from the blasting in the mines!"

Meanwhile, at the other end of the train, Stuart and the local police were attempting to handle matters. It was certainly an understatement to say that Stuart had become immensely popular with the miners in the last twenty-four hours. News of his meeting earlier that day with the other owners in his Iron Cliffs office had leaked out somehow, as well as Stuart's speech to them. This accounted in part for his influence with the miners during this particularly critical time. Therefore, he successfully appealed to the men to support the police as they approached and arrested the man who had thrown the ore at the officer of the troops. The arrest was made without any resistance on the part of the miners who were at the end of the train. While that was happening, Stuart prevailed on the men to bring back the engine and couple it to the rest of the train.

The wounded officer had been taken to the hotel and Dr. Saxon had been summoned. Stuart assured the officer now in command that he would be personally responsible for his well-being. The miners, along with their four hundred new "recruits," began marching into the square with the new men in the middle. The agent of the mine owners, who had been in sheer terror for his life during all the excitement and was hiding behind one of the seats in the coach that had brought in the troops, stepped onto the platform, cursing the entire situation. The officer in command firmly asked what the agent planned to do now.

In reality there was nothing to do but to return with the handful of remaining men. The idea of attempting to get the others back while they were surrounded by a mob was not a pleasant one to entertain, so the agent came to that conclusion quite quickly. The officers and troops then climbed into the coaches, and the train started down the range of hills. A tremendous cheer went up from the miners as the train disappeared. The whole episode had taken less than twenty minutes, but to Stuart it seemed like an hour. He was growing old very fast since his father had died, leaving him his millions.

It still seemed to him that he was at the very beginning of this problem, and that each event only complicated the situation. He could not foresee the outcome, but his heart was at peace because of his newly found life. Even in all the excitement, his new life proved to be the most triumphant part of his consciousness. In mulling it over later he recalled with great pleasure the fact that at the very moment he had jumped between the miners and the guns that were trained on him, he had said to himself, "I am a disciple of Christ. If I die, I will be with Him in paradise."

He made his way through the different groups of miners crowding into the square and went into the hotel. He wanted to inquire about the officer. Andrew Burke had gone on before him. The hotel manager escorted Stuart into the room where the man had been carried. The doctor had just arrived.

Stuart went in, and the first person to meet him was Andrew. He had been one of the men who had helped carry the unconscious officer from his ranks. Kneeling by the side of the wounded man was the leader of the Salvation Army. She had very quickly begun to treat the wounded man, and the moment the doctor saw the man, he grumbled something about its being the proper treatment.

Yet he quickly went to work, accepting the help of the young woman as if it were routine. Stuart and Andrew silently stood nearby, assisting whenever the doctor asked for something. "He'll never want his photograph taken again," the doctor grimly remarked as he finally ceased his work, but only after doing everything in his power to help the man. "This strike is bringing me a lot of unsolicited work. I guess I can send my bill to the state for this patient, but if the troops begin firing guns at the miners, I'll go bankrupt sewing them up and sawing off their arms and legs for nothing. Thank you, madam," the doctor said, turning to the woman in the Salvation Army uniform as she calmly looked at the officer who was still unconscious. "You were a great help. You've been a nurse before, or I'm mistaken."

"Yes, sir, I served a full term in Bellevue."

The doctor looked at her with even more respect. "You have the touch of a lady," he said politely. That was the height of a compliment from him.

"I am one," replied the young woman somewhat shyly. Stuart thought she smiled faintly. Her face was usually serious, but at times it could be remarkably winsome as her personality suddenly began to brighten.

The doctor coughed to hide his embarrassment at her reply, and then said, "I would be glad to introduce you to these two gentlemen here, lady." Then after an embarrassing hesitation, he added, "If I knew your name."

"I am Rhena Dwight. I'm presently here in Champion with the Army," she answered with perfect self-confidence.

"This is Mr. Duncan, the owner of the Champion mines; and this is Reverend Burke, the minister of St. John's," the doctor said, turning toward Stuart and Andrew.

She turned and bowed quietly, while the doctor checked on his patient again.

"You are Miss Dwight, the daughter of Allen Dwight!" exclaimed Stuart eagerly. The moment he spoke he wished he could retract his words.

However, his exclamation seemed to affect the young woman only for a moment. Then she answered, "Yes, Allen Dwight is my father." She added, while a slight bit of color swept over her pale face, "You were quite a brave man today, Mr. Duncan. I want to thank you on behalf of the poor men who seemed so much like sheep without a shepherd. How Christ would have looked on them with compassion!"

She gazed through the window past Stuart, who was standing near it. The square was crowded with the men, and someone had climbed to the stage and was speaking. As never before, Stuart saw the crowd with mixed emotions. The large unguided multitude was sad, yet thrilling, and for the first time he felt able to see them through Christ's eyes.

He also felt a sense of excitement at having met Rhena Dwight. She turned to the doctor and in a whisper asked a question. The doctor nodded his head and she left. After realizing she would not return and after seeing that everything possible was being done for the wounded officer, Stuart started for home.

On the way he took the time to recall what he knew about

Rhena—facts that the excitement of recent days had temporarily crowded from his mind. Some three years before, while Stuart was in college, Allen Dwight's daughter had surprised and astounded the high society of New York by suddenly deciding to leave her home and her fashionable surroundings to join the Salvation Army. He remembered the sensational accounts that appeared in the papers. Above all, he vividly recalled the effect of the news on her brother, who at the time was a classmate of Stuart. He could also remember talking it over with Louise when he came home for his Christmas vacation.

Louise seemed shocked by the news—at least as much as she had a capacity to be shocked by anything. She just could not grasp how any girl with such a promising career ahead of her, and who had such musical talent and social skills, could give them up, simply to throw her life away in the slums for some horribly dirty, drunken, and miserable people. "She must be crazy," Louise had said. "Her father is right in saying, if the report is true, that Rhena can never enter his home again as his daughter." His family's aristocratic connections had been deeply disgraced by the episode, and his personal standing in society was under scrutiny. He felt the shame of it with great bitterness, and he never wanted to speak of it.

Stuart continued thinking of Rhena as he neared home. He had never met her before and knew nothing of her reasons for such a complete change in her life. Yet he thoughtfully wondered if her reason had been an experience like what he had experienced earlier today.

Louise greeted him with the news that Aunt Royal, whom they had expected to be on the noon train, had telegraphed that she had stayed home another day due to the trouble that was likely to follow the arrival of the troops. Ross Duncan's sister had planned for some time to visit Louise and to stay throughout the winter if Louise wanted her to do so.

"Eric has been calling for you, Stuart. He's quite nervous. Life's not been worth living since all this excitement began over these labor troubles!" Louise said sharply. "Once Aunt Royal arrives, I want us to focus on something besides all this."

Stuart did not reply and went to see Eric. Meanwhile, Louise walked into the living room and banged on the piano as hard as she could. She was angry with Stuart and with everything else in general.

"Well, old friend," said Stuart cheerfully, "we had an exciting time. But no one's been killed yet, and I think the worst is over."

"Tell me about it." Eric tried to sit up a little and nervously moved his fingers over his blanket.

Stuart briefly described the scene at the train, and Eric listened with a tense and furrowed brow.

"That Salvation Army girl must be a brave one. Who did you say she was?"

"Rhena Dwight. She has just come here, I understand, within the last day or two." Stuart went on to tell Eric her story as he knew it, and Eric listened with great eagerness. Then he inquired about the miners. He asked how they had behaved, what they were planning to do, what the next move would be, and whether the new workers who had gone down to the lower range of hills would go into the mines or whether they would be stopped by the miners.

After they had bantered back and forth with questions and answers for several minutes, Eric said, "I tell you, Stuart, I've got to get out of this bed—and soon! The doctor can't make me stay here for two weeks. I'll get someone to carry me to the square if I can't walk. Now is the very time I ought to be with the men. If they begin to break the law, the cause of labor will suffer a setback that it will not recover from for years."

"That's true, Eric. But there is a lawlessness already awakened in the men that is growing worse every day. If a gun had been fired this afternoon, I doubt if even one of the troops would have left the place alive. The men would have crawled over a hundred dead bodies to tear the soldiers to pieces. I don't believe I've ever come so close to seeing the claws of a wild beast rising up in a mob in all my life."

"Yes," sighed Eric sadly, "well, I've seen those claws more than once. And I trust that heaven will grant that you never have to see them." He was referring to the events that had occurred when he was a boy in the coal regions of England. He and Stuart had talked about them often in times past.

"Amen," answered Stuart. Then he remained silent, for his mind was busy pondering the events of the morning. He was hoping for the perfect opportunity to tell Eric about his experience at the beginning of the day. In the midst of the perplexing and complicated situation, Stuart kept thinking how his attitude toward the events in his life had been so dramatically changed. What had taken place must have been quite momentous to hold such a preeminent place in his mind.

At that moment Louise walked by the door, calling out as she entered the dining room, "Lunch is ready!" Stuart had forgotten all about eating, but he left Eric to eat and to keep Louise company.

The entire time he was eating he felt he should tell his sister about his—what should he call it? The word *conversion* had always been distasteful to him. But what had happened to him? It was certainly something remarkable—so remarkable that it had gripped and held him in a loving and joyful grasp. And he felt that every other concern of his life paled when compared to it. He was not an emotional person, and his education and training were such that he had always prided himself in being a refined and self-controlled man of the world. He told the truth and believed in clean living and in being strictly honest and brave. Yet he never exhibited any passion or feeling, except in rare moments when he would have a strange outburst of rage that seemed to sweep away his convictions as if he were a madman. He had always blamed these outbursts on heredity.

But now he felt as if a new passion had taken hold of him, and a new life controlled his entire being. He was completely calm and was thrilled with his new existence. There were no yesterdays anymore. Everything was today and tomorrow. Jesus was the one great central, throbbing, pulsing, moving impulse with him. He was a new man. And yet people continued to proclaim, from their shallowness, that the days of miracles were past. Could there be a greater miracle in all the earth than when a human being like Stuart Duncan is born again—becomes a new person in Christ Jesus?

By the time lunch was over Stuart had determined what to do. He must tell Louise. There must be a frank and perfect understanding between them on this matter. It was too important to be neglected, passed over, or postponed.

"Louise," he said as they went into the living room together, "I want to tell you something while we're alone."

Louise did not reply, so Stuart continued. However, he felt the gap between his sister and his new life to be wider and deeper with every word he uttered. "Early this morning I had a very remarkable experience. I had what seemed like a vision of my real life, and it revealed to me that all these years I've been neglecting the most important part of my life." Stuart hesitated a moment as Louise sat looking at him in silent astonishment. "This morning I decided, Louise, to become a Christian."

There was an embarrassing silence. Louise's face reddened as she looked away from Stuart. She said in a quiet voice, "What do you mean?"

Stuart did not know what to say at first. He felt that Louise would not understand him, but he spoke with all the directness and simplicity seemingly demanded by the occasion.

"I mean, Louise, that I'm going to live a new life, with God's help. I now see everything differently. I never used to think of Christ as anyone more than a historical figure. Now He seems like a personal friend to me. More than that, He seems to be my own personal Savior. I never really knew before what the words *saved* and *salvation* meant, but now they are real. They apply to my condition. I seem to look at all the events of life, my own and others, in the light of eternity. It is difficult for me to make all this clear to you, Louise. Would you understand it better if I used the old word *conversion,* and if I said that I had an experience this morning that has converted me to a Christian life?"

"No, I don't know that I would," Louise replied coldly. She had walked to the piano and sat down on the stool, facing Stuart. She would not look at his face.

"Can't you understand me, Louise?" cried Stuart. His disappointment was very great, although he had tried to prepare himself for something like this before he spoke.

"No, I don't understand, Stuart. It's strange to me that you don't believe you've been a Christian all this time. And now you speak as if I'm not one."

"Are you, Louise?" asked Stuart gently. But the question angered her more than he would have dreamed. He was very sorry he had even asked it. It had come across as if he were judging her by his own Christian experience, and that not yet a day old.

"Yes, I am! What do you think I am? A heathen?" Louise stamped her foot as she always did when she was angry. Stuart realized that her definition of the word *Christian* was different from his. He remained silent, while Louise spun around on the piano stool and fitfully banged out a few chords. Then she wheeled around and said bluntly, "What are you going to do? Join the Salvation Army?"

Stuart fell back in his chair as if struck by a fist. It all seemed so contrary to his early-morning experience that he was completely unable to shape his thoughts into words. He was silent until Louise repeated her question.

"I guess I'll join St. John's Church. And I may join the Salvation Army too. I've heard that you can do that without actually becoming part of the ranks."

Louise rose to her feet with a look of scorn that Stuart could hardly bear. "Well, Father ought to be here to see all this! He would want to know if this was really Stuart Duncan, his son."

"It is true he would not see the old Stuart Duncan," replied Stuart with a noble dignity that even Louise could not help noticing. "But he would find a better one, I hope. Louise, I wish you could understand exactly what I have felt. It is impossible for me to look at things as I did before. I wanted you to know this now, so that you will not be surprised by what may happen in the future."

"What do you mean? Are you referring to joining the Salvation Army? I suppose their new leader is attracting you. I understand Rhena Dwight has been sent here to take charge."

It was as cruel and harmful an accusation as Louise could think of to say. She had become quite bitter by the events of the past few days, and more than once she had satisfied her own selfishness by delighting in making Stuart suffer.

Stuart's face, and even his lips, became pale. In spite of his Christian experience, or his conversion as he called it, at this point nothing was more sacred in his thoughts than the memory of the Army leader who had sacrificed and surrendered all that most young women would consider precious.

"Louise!" he cried. If he had not been in the grasp of a greater Power, he would have been swept into one of his old fits of anger. "Louise! You don't know what you're wounding here. Please don't try to harm my view of Christ or cast dishonor on His work in my forgiven soul! You have no right!"

He spoke so sternly, and yet with an evident right to defend his inner motives, that Louise was frightened. Perhaps she was close to asking Stuart's forgiveness, but he, not wanting to prolong the conversation, left the room to check on Eric. Louise stood quietly alone by the piano for a few minutes, and then finally went upstairs to her own room.

Stuart sat down by Eric and asked the nurse to leave them alone a little while. He was still smarting from his conversation with Louise, but he wanted to tell Eric of his experience. He seemed compelled to do so before another day had dawned.

In a very few sentences he told Eric of his experience that morning. Eric listened in total wonder. He was quite weak and grasped Stuart's hand, lightly squeezing it as he began to speak.

"You know, Stuart, to be honest, I've never experienced what our people call the 'leading of the Lord.' I joined the Army because I believed it was the only kind of Christianity that could really accomplish something."

"How can that be, Eric? Don't you have a personal relationship with Christ as your Savior?"

"Yes, I think I do. But it's not as evident to me as I would like."

"This is really astonishing to me," replied Stuart thoughtfully. "You know I've never even dreamed of talking about salvation or about a Savior. Do you remember? Have we ever talked about this subject before?"

Eric shook his head.

"Yet now," continued Stuart reverently, "I feel much different from what I've ever felt. I can't explain it, Eric, but Christ is the most real of all the realities in my life. Let me say it like this: from this point on I'm not willing or able to do anything without first asking, 'Would Christ approve this?' Would He say, 'Do it'?"

"Just one question then, Stuart. Does this also apply to the use of your property and money and this present labor dispute?" asked Eric bluntly.

"Yes!" The answer came with such positive conviction that it thrilled the pale face on the pillow. "Yes! My whole life is changed. All my relations with my fellowmen, all my possessions and their use, and any influence I have of any kind are now submissive to the law of my new indwelling life. Eric, do you believe that God actually makes His dwelling in man?"

Eric did not reply at once. There was a thoughtful silence.

"Yes, I believe it, but I don't see it very plainly. Yet if you really feel as you say you do, it will change how you respond to the miners and others in town."

"Yes, of course it will. I don't know all the details yet, but I'm willing to walk wherever the light shines. Eric, old friend, life even with the present troublesome crisis is a wonderful thing to me now."

"I'm glad for you," replied Eric simply.

Stuart realized that Eric could not handle much more, so he called for the nurse and soon left. That brief time of sharing did much good for the two men.

It was nearly three o'clock. Word was sent to Stuart that the men who had been persuaded to leave had gone back on the first train east. There had been a large demonstration and then the miners had disappeared from town, many of them going down to the lower range of hills to help the miners there in their dealings with the few remaining new workers.

Things were quiet in Champion as the day wore on, and there was no news of any problem from the lower range. The owners there had not tried to send the new workers into the mines, but were evidently waiting for a large contingent to arrive from the south and west. They would not pass through Champion.

Everything in town seemed to be on hold the following day at noon when Stuart's Aunt Royal arrived. She was a large and showy woman, who was a slave to high society. She was a woman of the world, a born diplomat, and a financier with very opinionated views of life. Not surprisingly, among her views was the conviction that you may as well be dead if out of fashion or banned from high society. She referred to people who were not at her level as "the masses" or "common people," if she ever deigned to mention them at all. She had inherited a large amount of money, a great deal of which was invested in tenements and saloon property in New York. Aunt Royal did not like for people to know that her primary means of support was the income from these properties, but it was a historical fact and something that could not be separated from her history. Besides, it was certainly not the poor who owned the saloons and tenements of New York and received the rent from them. In summation, Aunt Royal was very much like her brother, the late Ross Duncan, except for his gruff and harsh style of speech. She never spoke in a tone other than one that was sweet and gentle. Even a French revolution in the streets of New York would not have caused Aunt Royal to speak roughly or raise her voice. She had little education, since her father had been only a gardener in one of the city's suburbs. Yet it was there that he had begun to make his money. As a girl, she had helped him more than once by driving his wagon loaded with vegetables and fruit into the city. She never spoke of that now.

The first word Louise said upon seeing her was, "Aunt Royal, I hope you've come to stay all winter."

"I think so. Yes, I would be glad to escape the whirlwind of the city for a change this winter."

"We're having quite a little 'whirlwind' up here, madam," remarked the doctor, who had come up to see Eric that afternoon and was standing in the hall where Louise had greeted her aunt.

"Ah, Dr. Saxon!" said Aunt Royal. "I'm delighted to see you again." In reality she vigorously hated the doctor, and the doctor returned her feelings with compounded interest. "I assume you're referring to the labor trouble up here. I suppose it will quiet down again soon. These people will soon be forced back to work again. They never accomplish anything with these uprisings."

"You're right. They only accomplish more work for the doctors," replied Dr. Saxon. He went into Eric's room, and Aunt Royal and Louise went upstairs.

"So you have one of these labor people in the house? Don't you consider that rather dangerous?" Aunt Royal questioned in her sweet, clear voice as she was going up the broad staircase with her niece.

Eric heard every syllable distinctly as he lay in his bed. He had met Aunt Royal once, and the meeting was not a pleasant memory for him. He had never been able to keep from choking when he thought of the condescending air with which the woman had spoken to him the day he had saved Stuart's life. It was as if he had been a Newfoundland dog that she had patted on the head for pulling Stuart from the water with his teeth.

"When do you think I can get out of here, Doctor?" he asked almost roughly.

"Not for a week, anyway. You're doing well. And don't mind her. I'd hate to have the job of being her family physician. I don't believe she has a real heart. It's a piece of leather with valves, designed to let only a small amount of blood through with every beat. She has no more circulatory system than a frog."

Eric stared at the doctor. He had never heard the doctor, even at his angriest, say anything so harsh. The doctor seemed ashamed immediately and tried to apologize by saying, "I shouldn't have said that, but I feel better for having said it."

Two days passed, but the situation between the mine owners and the strikers remained nearly the same. The owners on the lower range of hills had not yet succeeded in getting enough new men to go to work, and several that had gone from Champion to work had already been persuaded to leave. The troops were still at the DeMott mine, and the miners' speeches in their daily meetings at the park were growing increasingly bitter toward them. The wounded officer in the hotel was recovering. Some of his friends had arrived to take care of him, and the doctor predicted he would be well enough to leave by the end of the week. Andrew Burke was becoming a wonderful friend to the officer. He had taken some of his very best roses to brighten the room and had himself proved the truth of the proverb, "A merry heart does good like medicine."

That Friday night the Vasplaines had invited Aunt Royal, Louise, and Stuart to a quiet dinner at their house. Stuart did not want to go, for he knew who would be there. He had no liking for the son of Mr. Vasplaine, who for a year or so had been trying to strike up a relationship with Louise. Even before his recent life-changing experience he had never sought any contact with him, other than that of a casual acquaintance, because he knew enough about him to dislike his immoral conduct and his general character as a man.

The family was extremely wealthy, and except for the Duncans' house, theirs was the finest in Champion. It was situated at the other end of the valley toward the park. The elder Vasplaine had retired some years before, and his brother and son had continued running his lumber and copper businesses north of Champion. They were not directly involved with the iron mines, except as they affected the general business climate. So, of course, they were feeling the effects of the widespread strike.

Also in their family was a daughter, Una Vasplaine, a young woman about Louise's age. The girls had been classmates together. Stuart was sitting by Una at the dinner, and the conversation was general in nature, but all about him. She was somewhat teasing him for looking so serious that night. Una was a vivacious girl with a striking appearance, and Stuart had always enjoyed his conversations with her in the past. He smiled in response to her teasing and was about to reply when something shocking happened, causing the ladies to scream and propelling the men to their feet in alarm.

The large dining room faced the front porch of the house, and a magnificent plate glass window extended from the floor to the ceiling, providing a view of the pine-covered lawn. The night was clear and chilly. It was growing late in the season so the ground was now bare and dry, and winter would soon arrive. The moon was just coming up over the Davis Hill range.

Suddenly through the huge window came a large chunk of iron ore, sailing over the table. It scattered the glass in every direction and even crashed into the glass of the electric chandelier. It smashed into the mirror over the sideboard, splintering it into a million pieces, and then fell onto the sideboard itself, breaking all the glasses and dinnerware.

The cruel event was so unexpected, coming with no warning at all, that they were totally terrified and shocked. Aunt Royal was the first to speak. "This is the work of some of your precious strikers."

"I don't believe it!" Stuart shouted. In his heart he hated the saloon for all the wickedness and heartache it caused. He believed the ore had been thrown by a rum-crazed person.

The men rushed onto the porch, while the elder Vasplaine, thoroughly incensed by the outrage, ordered his horses brought around. As soon as they were ready he and his brother started down the road in pursuit, and to notify the Champion police force of the crime. The younger Vasplaine volunteered to escort the ladies home, so Stuart hurried to town to investigate the incident. He did not believe any of the miners would do such a thing. Anything they had ever done to turn the owners against them had been done only when they were under the influence of alcohol. Besides, the Vasplaines were not mine owners now, although they had been some years before.

Stuart found everything to be quiet in the town. Most of the miners were still in DeMott, but the rumor was that a large group of men were coming in tonight. He stayed at the office for a little while, and then headed for home.

Walking out to the street, he saw the Salvation Army. They were kneeling at the corner for an outdoor meeting, just before going to their hall to hold their regular service. Rhena Dwight was kneeling on the hard stones of the pavement offering a prayer. Stuart could not hear her words, but he could see the pale, yet earnest face. He hesitated there for a moment, thought about going on home, but decided he would go to their hall to see what their meeting was like. As the Army finally stood and marched up the street to a drumbeat, Stuart slowly turned and walked in the same direction.

If he had not been so absorbed by his present surroundings as he entered the hall, he might have heard a sound carried from DeMott across the frosty ground by the clear mountain air. It was the sound of thousands of feet pounding the earth, heading toward Champion.

6

a
memorable
night

The Salvation Army Hall was formerly an old storage room, which had once been used for miners' supplies. It seated about four hundred people. There was very little furniture in it except for wooden chairs and two iron stoves, one at each end. A flag was draped across one corner. There was a platform about two feet above the floor where the Army was gathering for the meeting as Stuart entered the building.

Although many of the miners had gone over to DeMott that day in anticipation of the excitement that might take place once the new workers arrived, a large number of men were still in Champion. The Army had captured the curiosity of the town during the strike, so the hall was crowded tonight. Even the standing room was taken, except near the rear door and down the aisle, which by normal practice was left open so converts could walk down and kneel at the altar. The man with the bass drum was stationed at the end of the platform, but had difficulty finding enough room to swing his arm as he desired. And once during the evening as he pulled his arm back to strike the drum during a hymn of praise, he struck an interested spectator squarely on the nose. The minor incident created a little confusion, but it was soon quieted.

Stuart was familiar with their outdoor meetings, and he had seen the Army in their huge meetings in London, but it was different this time. In his present condition, and at this point of his personal history and experience, he looked at this particular meeting with increasingly keen and special interest.

He was sitting about six rows from the front and next to the aisle, where he could see everything clearly. The audience was mostly men, though several of the miners' wives and some younger women were scattered throughout the crowd. The service started with a lively solo and chorus. The major, a large, round-faced Englishman with a voice that shook the windows, began with the song:

> *I was a deep-dyed sinner,*
> *Just as deep as I could be.*

The Army then responded with a stirring chorus to the Bowery tune of "Swim out, O'Grady!" The verse and chorus went like this:

> *I was a deep-dyed sinner,*
> *Just as deep as I could be;*
> *But, praise God for salvation,*
> *Today I know I'm free!*
> *I have God's smile upon me now,*
> *Of hell I have no fears;*
> *When the devil comes and tempts me*
> *Why, I whisper in his ears:*

Chorus.

Get out, Mephisto!
I have no use for you;
I'm a soldier in the Army,
And to Jesus I'll be true;
I'm fighting 'neath the colors,
The yellow, red, and blue.
Get out, old devil, get out!

They then sang the last of the five verses and the final chorus as follows:

A word about the collection,
For we want a good one, sure;
The devil often tells me
That to give I am too poor;
Which makes me go down deeper
When the timbrel comes my way,
And my action brings a blessing, sure,
And helps me when I say:

Second Chorus.

Get out, old devil!
I've lost my love for you;
I'm a soldier in the Army,
And to Jesus I'll be true;
I'm fighting 'neath the colors,
The yellow, red, and blue.
Get out, old devil, get out!

It would be impossible to describe the effect of this song on the audience. The Cornish people were great lovers of music, so before the large soloist had finished even two verses, nearly every foot in the audience was beating time on the hardwood floor. And by the conclusion of the third verse nearly every person in the hall was roaring out the words of the chorus with the Army, although they had not been invited to sing along.

The Army did not seem disturbed in the least, however. It would certainly take more than that to disturb the Salvation Army of Champion. At the conclusion of the song everybody on the platform knelt down.

Rhena Dwight was in the center of the little group. The audience was as quiet now as it had been noisy earlier. A smoky kerosene lamp was just above her head, and as she knelt there in the midst of those rough surroundings, Stuart could not help thinking who she once had been and who she was today. Her face was remarkable—refined, but elegant. It had seen great trouble, but through it all had seen great victory. Her prayer today was much like what Stuart had previously heard from her. The Army broke in frequently with "Amen!" and "Hallelujah!" but not noisily or in a way that was meant to interrupt. Stuart glanced here and there at the crowd, and saw tears running over the rough cheeks of many men and women. Then he bowed his own head, and when the prayer was finished and he lifted his face again, his own eyelashes were wet with tears.

Immediately after Rhena's prayer, a half dozen short prayers were offered by different members of the Army. Then they rose to their feet again, while one of the young ladies stepped to the front of the platform and began singing with only tambourine accompaniment. As she sang, two other Army members passed tambourines through the audience as collection trays. A meager contribution of pennies rattled onto their parchment covers while she loudly sang with great determination the following song and chorus:

Oh! I'm glad I am converted
In the Army of the Lord;
Oh! I'm glad I am converted
In the Army.

Chorus.

Reign, oh, reign! My Savior!
Reign, oh, reign! My Lord!
Send the sanctifying power
In the Army of the Lord,
Send the sanctifying power
In the Army.

He will give you grace to conquer
In the Army of the Lord;
He will give you grace to conquer
In the Army.

He will fill you with His Spirit
In the Army of the Lord;
He will fill you with His Spirit
In the Army.

Oh! I feel the power is coming
In the Army of the Lord:
In the Army.

At that point of the service Rhena began to speak. And as long as Stuart lives he will never forget his feelings as he listened or the impression her words made upon the rough, uncultured audience. Where had this young woman, raised in the showcase atmosphere of high society and trained to be refined and exhibit artificial politeness, caught the spirit that knows how to relate to people of the street, the mines, and poor and hardworking homes? She had certainly caught it, and the old storage room, with its audience of strong and hardened, rough men and women, was now the scene of a strange victory of spirit over spirit. Rhena's voice was a wonderful gift. It was very clear and strong for such a little body. It penetrated the souls of the people, but it was what she said that held them like captives bound to her will. She spoke simply, lovingly, and with true enthusiasm of the great love of God in sending His Son into the world. It was not preaching, but was a message of one saved soul to others who were still in peril. She spoke only a few minutes, and as she closed, she asked those who were under conviction of sin to come forward and kneel by the platform.

Immediately, an older man stumbled into the aisle. He was somewhat under the influence of liquor and kept bumping into people on either side of the aisle. If it had not been for the friendly nudges of those people, it is doubtful he would ever have succeeded in making it to the platform. He did reach it, however, and knelt down, resting his head and arms on the platform at Rhena's feet. Instantly, in a voice that thrilled every ear in the room, Rhena started the song:

> *Return, O wanderer, return,*
> *And seek your Father's face;*
> *Those new desires that in you burn*
> *Were kindled by His grace.*

Return, O wanderer! Return;
  He hears your humble sigh;
He sees your softened spirit mourn,
  When no one else is nigh.

Return, O wanderer! Return;
  Your Savior bids you live;
Come to His Cross, and you will learn
  How freely He'll forgive.

As she finished each verse, the Army chimed in with the chorus:

Oh, you must be a lover of the Lord,
Or you can't go to heaven when you die.

The contrast between the absolutely cultivated voice singing the verses and the noisy, drum-accompanied rattle of the chorus startled Stuart, causing him to wince each time the chorus was sung. Yet Rhena did not seem disturbed in the least by it. She smiled at the enthusiastic swinging of the arm that pounded the big drum and nodded her head to the beat of the chorus as the audience joined in.

Several persons went forward and knelt during the song. At its conclusion the major, who seemed to be in charge of the service this evening, asked for testimonies. Nearly every member of the Army on the platform shared a brief and simple message that was listened to in complete silence by the audience. Each message, however, was followed with the clapping of hands. The testimonies generally consisted of a statement something like this: "Two months ago I found Jesus right here in this room. Praise His name! He is very precious to my soul."

"The Lord spoke to me of His cross just three weeks ago tonight, and I gave Him my heart. Hallelujah!"

"I was a drunken, worthless sinner a year ago. Yet now I am redeemed, washed in the blood of the Lamb, and I am not ashamed to testify of His salvation."

"Before I was converted and joined the Army, I was known as 'Crusty Joe, the whiskey soak.' Now I'm a new man, and haven't had a nip for more than a month. My name is Joseph now, and don't you forget it! Amen!"

One of the recent women converts came forward and, in a trembling voice and with tears streaming down her cheeks, said, after waiting for the laughter following Crusty Joe's testimony to cease, "Until a short time ago I was an outcast on God's earth. The Army found me and told me of the love of Jesus. I'm redeemed and all my sins have been washed away in His precious blood. Glory be to His name!"

As Stuart sat there listening, a great torrent of feeling overcame him. It rose in him like a swelling tide, and he did not try to repress it. There was something very wonderful to him in the crude, rough, and simple way in which these common men and women spoke of forgiven sins and their personal Savior. Some of their words were different, yet each testimony was like his experience of only a few days before. And although speaking to this group was the last thing in the world he would have expected to do when he had entered the hall, it now seemed very natural—even necessary. So acting under what he believed to be the leading of a divine impulse, he stood to speak. With all the people in the audience and on the platform looking at him, and in the midst of silence that seemed nearly painful to him, he began, "My friends, I want to say with these other saved souls that I have also lately felt God's hand upon me. I acknowledge Jesus Christ to be my personal Savior, and with His help I want to live a life as His disciple."

It was a very simple, unemotional statement, which was entirely devoid of any pride regarding his conversion. But it had a profound effect upon everyone in the hall. Rhena Dwight reddened, then turned pale again, and her lips silently moved as if she were offering a prayer. The members of the Army remained motionless, while the older miners who had known Stuart from boyhood stared at him as if he were another person. And indeed he was!

He was still standing in the same spot with everyone focused on him when the silence of the room was broken by the sound of a swarm of marching feet. It seemed to be a deliberate, heavy sound, and instantly, every man in the room was standing. Someone near the door shouted to those in the room, "There's been a fight down at DeMott! They're bringing soldiers up here."

In the next moment every man in the room was stampeding toward the crowded door. Stuart was near the platform, and it seemed the most natural thing in the world, in spite of the sudden confusion caused by the unceremonious exit of the audience, that he would be talking with Rhena Dwight. In the midst of the noise of overturning chairs and the tumultuous crowd just outside the door of the hall, he told her of his experience earlier that week. He related how for the first time in his life he had felt the personal touch of God's divine power, and had heard the call to his soul from the living and risen Christ, "Follow Me." Somehow it seemed to be the most natural thing in the world to be sharing a part of his inner life with this small, yet resolute woman in the Salvation Army uniform. Rhena clasped her hands together as her eyes glistened with tears.

"Thank you, Mr. Duncan, for telling me," she said simply.

Their conversation had taken only a few minutes. Then after speaking to some of the other members of the Army, who each offered him a hearty "God bless you, sir," Stuart started to leave. Halfway down the aisle, he turned and hurried back to Rhena, and said, "Miss Dwight, I hope you will not risk your life in the crowd tonight. I don't know what the men are going to do, but you have been too daring already. I beg you—please do not venture out among the miners tonight."

He did not wait to hear her reply. She looked surprised, and as he left, he wondered if his words had sounded more like a command than a request. Yet as soon as he was outside, he became absorbed by what he saw in the square—the scene of so much of the town's recent excitement.

As he considered the facts surrounding the strike, he wondered if things were rapidly coming to a head that would lead to some kind of tragedy tonight. These were his thoughts even before he learned that earlier in the evening, while he had been at the Vasplaines' and the Salvation Army Hall, the miners at DeMott had become involved in a violent conflict with the troops. During the fight that had taken place the troops had fired their weapons, killing two of the men and wounding several others. Before another round could be fired, however, the miners had completely overwhelmed the troops and disarmed them.

After a brief but fiery debate the miners were determined to exact vengeance in keeping with the tragedy. They had tied the hands together of each man in both units of the troops, placed them in the center of the crowd, and marched them across the hills into Champion. Once there the plan was to allow the mob to give them a short trial and then to shoot their officers. They had marched them back to Champion because the two miners who had been killed were from there. Their bodies were brought with the crowd, carried into the square, and placed at the foot of the stage. The captured men and officers stood together directly in front of the dead bodies, while a huge crowd of miners filled all the remaining space around the stage.

Stuart learned what had happened as soon as he walked onto the street. As he absorbed the terrible news, his heart grew sick. He had never seen the Cornishmen, the Danes, the Norwegians, and the few Italians of Champion so united on anything in all his life. They were possessed with the thought of vengeance. The moon had fully risen and was flooding the square with its mellow light. It was quite chilly, but there was not even a breath of wind. Stuart could never have imagined the possibility of such a scene in his hometown. A dozen men had climbed to the stage and the tragedy was about to begin. They were moving ahead with a public trial of the troops, which was to be followed by a predetermined shooting of at least half a dozen of them.

For a moment Stuart remained motionless, smitten with silent hopelessness. The whole town was in the grasp of the mob and the handful of police was powerless. What could possibly thwart the torrent that was about to be unleashed, and where would it end? The only hope of additional troops was in Hancock, one hundred miles away. Before they could arrive, the tragedy would be ended.

Stuart groaned inside as he longed for Eric's presence and influence. Nevertheless, he had almost instinctively jumped into the crowd to raise his lone voice against the impending horror. Just as he did so, someone pulled him from behind, nearly knocking him from his feet. Dr. Saxon had leaned from his buggy to grab Stuart, and then said to him, "Two of the biggest fools on earth are out here tonight, and if you will allow me to join you, we'll be a threesome that's hard to beat!"

"What! How's that?" cried Stuart in amazement. His surprise was doubled when the doctor removed the blanket covering Eric's deathly looking face as he lay on the seat next to him. "Eric! You're here!" It all seemed like a dream to Stuart.

"Quickly! If you're going to do something, do it with a bolt of lightning under it to speed it along!" exclaimed the doctor. He rapidly filled Stuart in with his story from earlier that evening. "I was in DeMott tonight when the trouble occurred. I drove back here and came around by the Beury road past the house. I stopped for a minute to see Eric, and when I told him the men were marching into Champion with the troops, he swore by all his old Anglo-Saxon gods that he must come down here and talk to them. So here he is. It'll probably kill him, but he said if I wouldn't bring him down, he'd just get up and try to walk here. If he dies, it's suicide, not a case of malpractice. Yet perhaps he'll pull through, for in spite of all my doctoring I can't seem to kill off even one of these labor agitators. Here! Help him out, Stuart. Confound him! Wouldn't you know he wants to get up there in the middle of the high priests of this strike till the last enemy is dead! Gently, now! I'll bet you a day's pay he'll faint straightaway before he can open his mouth to say his little speech!"

The seemingly tough words were all from a doctor who was assisting Stuart in lifting Eric from the buggy with great skill and tenderness. Eric was suffering tremendous pain, but motioned to the doctor and Stuart to carry him through the crowd.

All things considered, it was not surprising to see Eric there. Stuart realized what his presence might mean as he shouted to the miners around him to make room for Eric. The men were amazed to see their weak and wounded young leader being carried through the mob. They moved back, opening a path directly to the stage. Once there, Eric shouted with a strong voice that gave Stuart much hope regarding his recovery, "Straight up the stairs! Quickly! I'm able to speak to the men. Please, God, don't let them do this terrible wrong tonight."

Some of the men on the stage came partially down the crude steps to help Stuart and the doctor. After all, they did not yet know Eric's motive for being there, and they were still greatly influenced by him. They certainly had no thought of resisting any attempt he might make to address the crowd.

They carried Eric up to the stage, while the doctor and Stuart helped him to the front and propped him on his feet. He then looked over a scene that was to become a lifelong memory for them all.

The moon was full, so there was no need of torches or lamps. The two dead men had been placed on a crude platform of boards at the foot of the stage and elevated so that their bodies were visible to the miners, even those who were at a distance. Their uncovered faces stared straight upward in the cold midnight air. The captured soldiers were forced to stand directly in front of the bodies, and due to the size of the huge mob, several of them were so close to the ghastly platform that they were actually touching it. An eerie darkness seemed to hang over the entire square and its mob. Every face was hard and stern, with every eye now lifted toward Eric as he stood to confront them.

Only a very great man knows the way to the heart of a mob. There was probably not another soul in all of Champion that night who knew how to play the heartstrings of emotion and impulse as well as Eric Vassall. To Eric it was a question of dealing with the men he loved—men for whom he had voluntarily given up all other competing ambitions for their cause alone. He assumed the right to speak at this crisis point as one who had sacrificed more than anyone else for the sacred cause of labor. No one on the stage dared to deny him that privilege or to derail his purpose.

What can a man say on such an occasion? It is doubtful whether Stuart or the doctor, who heard every word, could have later told what Eric said. Every word burned like fire in the air, but they were not words easily repeated. The doctor was amazed at the power of Eric's voice, for it rang out like a trumpet and reached the farthest person. It meant, of course, he would probably collapse after the intense strain, so Dr. Saxon carefully watched for signs of it.

The thrust of Eric's appeal was centered on the need to preserve the sacred cause for which the men had sacrificed all that they had and were, and to keep it unblemished. The pleasure of tasting vengeance would last only a little while, yet the cause of labor would be dead forever, at least for them, if they broke the law by taking vengeance tonight. He appealed to their religious sensitivities, which he knew to be strong in hundreds of the men before him. He reminded them of the prayers that had been offered from the very place where he now stood. How could a just God or a merciful Savior look with anything but horror upon men who had vowed to love and obey Him, but who had plunged headlong into such a crime? Was the cause they represented more valuable than the lives of these men? Would revenge bring their brothers back to life? Which of these miners felt the wrongs and injustices more than he did? He clearly realized that this crime of passion would break the thin bond of sympathy that united them with the general public. It would be a crime that would never be lessened in the eyes of mankind during his lifetime or that of his children's children.

Eric had never put so much of himself into an appeal before, and it had never cost so much. It would be a wonderful triumph for him if he could prevail tonight. And he believed he could see signs of yielding on the part of the men. If only he could hold out a little longer! He staggered in the arms of Stuart and the doctor as all his nerves seemed to throb with agonizing pain. The panoramic view of the square floated before him in a mist of moonlight, and the dull murmuring of the mob broke over his ears like the surf on a faraway coast. He felt his voice failing him, his tongue seemed like ashes in his mouth, but he felt he must continue.

Eric began to feel earth and heaven slipping away from him. The men had listened in wonderful silence, yet Eric had not completed his heart's desire, nor had his words performed their work in the minds of the men, which he hoped would appeal to their conscience and reason.

At that very moment, a voice rose above the crowd from the steps of the Salvation Army Hall, which comprised one corner of the square in Champion near the railway station. It was the voice of Rhena Dwight and she was not speaking, but singing.

Since coming to Champion and having contact with the miners and their families, Rhena had learned how much the Cornishmen cherished their music and were influenced by it. It was not such a remarkable thing, therefore, that as she stood and listened to Eric that night, she was led to use the gift that God had given her. More than once she had seen angry passions calmed and brute impulses thwarted by the sound of her voice. As Eric weakened, Rhena, moved by a true leading of God, broke into a song that soared like an angel's over the hushed and wondering crowd. Oh, if only more of us might be sensitive to follow God's leading in that way!

The clear, chilly air carried every word and note to the ears of the thousands of men who stood packed into the square. The distance was not very great, her voice was trained, and her enunciation was distinct and exact; but the ability to evoke a feeling of compassion, as well as the plea and warning that rose from Rhena, could have been sung only with the help of God's divine power. It is He who takes and uses our poor and weak human powers to His glory when they submit themselves to His will for His service. She sang these words while the mob listened:

> *It's true there's a beautiful city,*
> *That its streets are paved with gold;*
> *No earthly tongue can describe it;*
> *Its glories can never be told.*
> > *But I know, I know!*
> > *I know I shall be there!*
>
> *Your loved ones dwell in that city,*
> *Whom you placed beneath the sod,*
> *When your heart felt nigh to breaking*

And you promised you'd serve your God.
  Will you? Will you?
  Say, will you meet me there?

There none but the pure and holy
Can ever enter in;
You have no hope of its glory
If still you're the servant of sin.
  Bless God! Bless God!
  Bless God, you may be there!

Yes, you can go there, my brother,
For Jesus has died on the tree;
And that same precious blood is flowing
That washed a poor sinner like me.
  Will you? Will you?
  Will you now wash and be clean?

All who enter that glorious city
Have made their garments of white,
Have trod in the Savior's footsteps;
They've battled for God and for right.
  I long, I long!
  I long to meet you there!

Never before had such a singer, audience, occasion, or purpose been used or influenced in such a mighty way by the divine passion of music. Long before she finished, Eric fainted dead away, and Stuart and the doctor were caring for him as he lay on the floor of the stage. His face was as ghastly white as the two bodies below. Stuart's senses throbbed to her song as they had never done before, even when compared to the triumphant arias he had heard in the golden, perfumed opera houses of Europe. How could those singers compare with this one who was using her gift to help save lives and prevent crime?

It was most likely the evening that Stuart Duncan laid his heart at the feet of Rhena Dwight. He had already surrendered his soul to God, and lifting up his heart to the height of loving this woman seemed a natural mingling of it with his recent spiritual experience.

Once the song had ended there seemed to be a sigh of relief from the men, as if they had been holding their breath during Rhena's singing. The crowd started to murmur, and the sound of it grew throughout the square, but the mob was not the same. An inner purpose had been deeply stirred in hundreds of the men. For the most part they were not cruel, brutal, or lawless men—to the contrary, many of them were deeply religious. Above all else they desired to see the cause of labor triumph. And the facts that Eric had so clearly presented were undeniable.

One of the older miners spoke from the stage. He knew the men had entered Champion with the intent of taking the law into their own hands, and he agreed with Eric and appealed for sober reasoning. He asked what would be accomplished by spilling the hot blood of the troops. A number of voices began crying out, calling for a union vote.

"Let the union decide!"

"We'll abide by the union's decision in the matter!"

So a vote was taken either to hand the soldiers over to the authorities to await due process of law or to allow the miners to deal with the troops for the deaths of the two men. The vote was taken by a show of hands, and less than a fourth of the men raised their hands, with clubs in them, to deal with the soldiers as they pleased. An overwhelming majority voted to submit the entire affair to the proper law authorities.

Immediately, everyone on the stage stepped down from the platform, including Dr. Saxon and Stuart, who helped carry Eric back to the doctor's buggy. Eric awakened somewhat from his fainting spell as he was being carried and asked to be taken to his own house. Although the doctor and Stuart thought it wiser to return to Stuart's, they reluctantly consented. After taking him home and making sure he was comfortable, Stuart then returned to the square.

The union vote was being faithfully carried out. The troops and their officers were under lock and key in the engine house, and the miners assisted the police of Champion in guarding them. The miners claimed that the troops had fired on them without excuse and that placing them under arrest was certainly just. And so ended a memorable night.

The very next day the troops were taken back to DeMott by the authorities, and a trial quickly followed. As the trial unfolded, it was determined that there was insufficient evidence to convict. The case against the soldiers was dismissed. The facts of the case showed that each side in the incident had been greatly provoked, although the miners would always consider the shooting to be unwarranted. They would always speak of the killing of the two men as murder and would forever continue to look upon the acquittal of the officer who gave the command to fire as an outrage and a clear miscarriage of justice.

On the night of the shooting Stuart finally returned to his home, feeling that the problem of the miners' strike was no closer to a solution. And he was greatly troubled by thoughts and emotions previously foreign to him. He found it hard to believe that the tremendous conflict had grown out of a struggle for a few cents more pay per day. As he watched the struggle unfold, he also found it more and more significant that human life was being risked around the clock for the cause of labor. He could not see the end in sight, and he dared not anticipate the final results.

As the days went by, the situation remained practically the same. The primary effect of sending the troops away was that the mine owners realized they had only a very slim chance of getting new men to work in the mines. The few new men who had gone from Champion to DeMott had gradually been persuaded to go back home, or they had begun looking for other work, since the owners had hesitated in forcing the issue of getting more new workers. In reality, the owners were concerned that if they were successful in putting new men to work, the local men would ruin the mines by flooding them. In addition, the price of ore was rapidly rising, and many owners had great quantities of ore in their stockpiles. Many people believed there was no great desire on the part of the owners to open the mines again as long as they had such large quantities of ore already at the top. Most thought the owners would be able to realize large profits even if the strike continued until spring and, therefore, would make even more money by not operating the mines.

Meanwhile, winter was quickly approaching, and the miners were finding it more and more difficult to get credit at the local stores. Many of the merchants refused to trust the men any longer, so the prospects of terrible suffering in Champion were quite real unless something were to dramatically change within the next couple of weeks.

Stuart began to seriously consider his own great wealth as a means of improving conditions in Champion. He had gone to visit Eric, who was now able to be up and around. While he was there Andrew Burke had also dropped by, and the three of them had begun to discuss possible ways of relieving the apparent distress of the miners and their families.

"I can't help feeling that this strike is all wrong, Eric," Stuart said, continuing the conversation by again focusing on the miners. "I receive letters every day from my agents in Cleveland, begging me to join the other owners in their refusal to grant the men their demand of two dollars a day. Every letter says that they do not see, even if the union would settle with only me, how I could possibly manage to operate the mine if held to my original decision to give two dollars a day per man."

"What are you going to do?" Eric asked.

"Only time will tell. Does the union show any signs of weakening?"

"Not yet, but there's no telling what will happen," said Eric with a sigh. "In fact, even my opinion of the strike is changing. Somehow I seem to have a different perspective on the future ever since my injury, especially since that night in the square."

"Does that mean you are more hopeful or less hopeful regarding the final result?" Andrew asked.

Eric remained silent for some time, thinking before he replied. "Well, at least in my lifetime, I don't expect to see what is right and the cause of brotherhood triumph, and I'll tell you why. The love of money is as old as civilization itself, and I can't think of a passion that is stronger or more enduring. It goes to the core of all human struggles and is the basis of every civilized person's life. Why, it's even woven into the fabric of the church! And the more I study the problem, the more I believe that nothing short of a massive financial earthquake will ever break civilization's grasp on gold and the love of wealth, the root cause of all the selfishness of the modern world as we know it today."

"There's no question that money is at the root of most of the world's selfishness," replied Andrew. "But its use has sometimes proved to be a blessing. I often think I could be a better person if I could pay off all my debts and buy all the roses I want."

"Yes, then you could be as selfish as the rest of us," said Stuart with a smile. Then returning to the problem at hand, he said, "What can we do about this current emergency situation? Regardless of how the men got themselves into it, I now understand that women and children are beginning to suffer. The cause is irrelevant at this point."

"Well, you've got plenty of money," Eric said bluntly.

"Yes, I do," Stuart quietly replied. Yet it was as if he were struck for the very first time with the awareness of the great power his wealth provided. The other two men curiously watched him—Eric from a workingman's perspective, and Andrew from the viewpoint of a minister.

"I'm ready to dedicate every cent I have to the good of humanity!" cried Stuart with enthusiasm. "And I want the two of you to show me how to do it wisely."

Eric stood, strolled toward the window, then returned to his chair, and remarked, "You really must be converted if it's gone as deeply as that!"

Andrew looked at Stuart and said smilingly, "If you really mean that, we'll need some time to think it over and formulate wise plans."

Stuart then stood and paced the little room. "I meant every word. When I became a Christian, I said in my heart, 'I will dedicate all I have and all I am to the cause of my Savior.' I fully understand what that means. I do not believe a man can be a Christian and allow money to be the great passion of his life. I believe he should think of himself as a steward or trustee in regard to money, and he should use whatever has been placed in his hands as God would have him use it. I don't know exactly how much money is at my disposal," he added, "but I would like for the three of us to form something of a 'ways and means' committee for the benefit of others in society. How does that idea strike the two of you?"

The three men agreed to meet the next day at Andrew's hotel and make definitive plans for their organization. Eric was able to get out again, although he was far from strong, and faced the prospects of very limited use of his weak shoulder for an indefinite period of time.

That afternoon Louise and Aunt Royal were at home discussing a party they were planning for the Vasplaines and three or four other families. Ross Duncan's death was still too recent for them to plan a large and elaborate party, so they were planning a simple, quiet dinner. Aunt Royal was very particular when it came to observing societal etiquette, especially when following it did not interfere with her own selfishness. When it did, however, she found that the rules of polite society allowed her to do whatever she wanted as long as she called it by the right name. She and Louise planned a quiet gathering, not a reception or a party, to which they had decided to invite twenty-five or thirty people representing the old and aristocratic families of Champion.

"Aunt Royal," Louise said after they had discussed what they would wear and eat at the gathering, "what do you think of inviting Rhena Dwight?"

"What!" she exclaimed. "The leader of the Salvation Army! What are you thinking of, child?"

"She is a beautiful singer," replied Louise. She seemed to be deep in thought.

"You mean you want to invite her simply to entertain our company?" asked Aunt Royal.

"Oh, I don't think she would come just to do that," replied Louise with a dry laugh.

"What made you think of inviting her then?" asked Aunt Royal with a searching look.

"Oh, never mind. It was just an idea," said Louise.

Later that afternoon Louise walked into town as she frequently did in the winter. She loved the exercise and believed it helped keep her well and attractive, so she persevered in it even in stormy weather.

Rhena Dwight rented a room from an elderly widow, who had two or three other boarders in her house just past the Salvation

Army Hall. After walking around the square, Louise passed the hall and knocked on the door of the rooming house. Rhena was in, and Louise was directed to her room. She knocked, and Rhena herself opened the door. She did not recognize Louise at first since the light in the hallway was quite dim. Once she finally recognized the face of the woman standing before her arrayed in a costly fur, she reddened ever so slightly. She asked Louise to enter and Rhena closed the door behind her. Outside, heavy snow was beginning to fall very quickly, and the short winter day was wrapping its twilight glow around the town of Champion.

7

plans
good
and bad

"Are you surprised to see me, Miss Dwight?" Louise asked, taking the seat Rhena indicated for her. "I am Louise Duncan, Stuart Duncan's sister."

"Yes, I know who you are. I've seen you walk past the Army Hall a number of times," said Rhena quietly, not having the remotest idea of the purpose of Louise's visit.

"We're going to have a little dinner party at our house next week, and we would be pleased if you could come," said Louise boldly, looking straight at Rhena. "I thought it would be less formal to drop by and invite you personally than to send a note."

Rhena looked at her caller with the utmost astonishment, for she did not know Louise at all. Even before leaving everything behind in high society to join the Army, she had never met her, and Rhena now thought Louise, who probably knew Rhena's past, might be thinking that she would enjoy a taste of her old life again. The face in the fur-trimmed hat looked very pretty, and Rhena warmed toward it.

"Thank you," she answered gently. "I appreciate your kindness, but it is impossible. I can't go because I've shut the door of my old life and do not want to open it again." She then fell silent as if memories claimed her thoughts. Finally, she added, with a smile that Louise could barely see through the unlit room, "Besides, I have my regular Army duties to perform every night. I can't leave my people, and there's a great need for visiting to be done now. The distress and suffering in miners' families are increasing very fast."

"I'm sorry you can't come," Louise said. She rose slowly to go, adding, "Stuart speaks of you occasionally, and I thought perhaps it would please him to invite you." Louise watched Rhena carefully, but her color did not change. She stood, instead, like a statue, pale and still. Louise continued, "I just thought you would probably feel like coming to our little informal gathering that we've planned. We've asked the Waltons, the Wymans, and the Vasplaines as well. Una and I are planning to do the honors in the music room since she plays so well, and we hoped you would accompany us with your beautiful voice."

"Una?" asked Rhena.

"Yes, Miss Vasplaine. It seems so natural for me to call her Una, of course. We were girls together growing up, and besides," added Louise with a short laugh, "since her recent engagement to my brother, Stuart, it seems more natural than ever. Well, I'm sorry you can't come. We would have enjoyed hearing you sing."

"You are kind to think of me, and I am grateful for it," replied Rhena. Her closest friend could never have detected any special emotion in her voice or her manner. With the lie about Stuart still fresh in her ears, she impressed even Louise. And even in those dingy surroundings and dressed in an Army uniform, she possessed an air of grace and refinement that few people could ever equal. Louise felt like making a casual remark about the difficulty of Rhena's lifework, but something about Rhena kept her from doing it. Instead, she left the room with the conventional words, "Good evening, Miss Dwight. So sorry you cannot attend our little gathering."

Once on the street again Louise mumbled to herself, "I was pretty sure she would refuse to come, but with that little tidbit of information about Una and Stuart, I don't think she'll continue to lead my brother on." She smiled, set her face toward home, and walked briskly through the fast-falling snow.

Anyone familiar with Louise Duncan would not be surprised by her visit to see Rhena Dwight or by her obvious lie regarding Stuart's engagement. The actions were a pretty accurate measure of her character and her petty and narrow views of life. She had observed enough of Stuart's actions lately to know that his feelings toward Rhena had become more than infatuation, and a relationship between them was the last thing in the world she wanted to see.

Louise would do anything, short of being caught in deception herself, to stop any association between her brother and the Salvation Army leader. So she had lied to Rhena. How would she ever know the difference? To be sure, Rhena was experienced in the ways of upper society, and if she had known Louise, she might have suspected something, but Stuart's sister had left her with the impression that she was a kindhearted person. Rhena also was grateful for Louise's apparent sincerity in recognizing her present position in Champion as still entitling her to a place in polite society.

Rhena did not light her lamp after Louise left, but sat by the window, looking out on the falling snow. Now that the weather had turned stormy the Army had moved their regular street meetings inside. When it was time for her to go to the Army Hall, she shivered in the cold. Her lips moved in words that would have been audible to a passerby: "O Lamb of God who takes away the sins of the world, pardon me and help me!" Very few people ventured out that evening, for the storm continued to grow throughout the night. By morning all of Champion, with its pine-covered hills, was deep with snow that swept past Rhena's windows and drifted into huge billows that were piled high against the old storage room door.

That afternoon Stuart trudged through the drifts to meet with Andrew and Eric as the three had agreed. They intended to plan for the relief of the miners, but wanted to arrange for something more permanent than a plan to simply meet the immediate distressing needs in Champion. In spite of his continuing weakness, Eric managed to get through the snow and insisted that the struggle did him good. Andrew welcomed them in his usual hearty fashion and immediately began to talk about his roses.

"Look at that! If that isn't a beauty, I don't know what is. Allow me to cut that one for you, Mr. Duncan."

"Not on your life! Not if you continue to call me 'Mister.' Have you forgotten our agreement?" Stuart replied, smiling.

Andrew looked somewhat puzzled and then said, "I just didn't know how Mr. Vassall here might take to me calling you by your first name, especially since he's such a longtime friend of yours."

"Eric," Stuart said, laying a hand on his old friend's shoulder, "do you object if Reverend Burke here calls me Stuart and I call him Andrew? It seems absurd that when a man saves another man's life, they should continue with such formal terms."

"My name is Eric then," he replied frankly. He was a man of many faults, but petty jealousy over Stuart's new friendship with Reverend Burke would not be one of them.

"That settles it then. It's to be Andrew, Eric, and Stuart from now on," Stuart eagerly asserted. He was filled with enthusiasm this afternoon, for he was passionate over this new idea of better using his money and power, and he felt able to do almost anything. Yet woven through his thinking about his newly consecrated money and its wonderful power was the glowing image of Rhena Dwight. His love for her was growing in strength and meaning every moment. He had not seen her since that night in the Army Hall, and he did not realize what a strong grasp his feelings toward her had on his entire being until now. As he faced this great opportunity, perhaps the greatest of his life, the slight form and pale face of the Salvation Army leader seemed to occupy a very prominent place in his mind.

Andrew cut off two of his choicest roses and gave one to Stuart and one to Eric.

"It seems a shame to cut those off the plants like that," Eric said as he took the flower and awkwardly stuck it in his lapel.

"But that's why I grow them," Andrew replied.

"How's your church work going?" asked Stuart, after thanking Andrew for the rose and then pulling himself from his deep thoughts.

"Oh, I don't know yet. It's taking a while to get acquainted and this is a new field for me. If I can succeed in making the people believe they like me, I think we'll have a good time together. I've never seen so many characters like this in all my life."

"Are you including us in that?" asked Eric.

"You bet I am! If I could, I'd write a book about the two of you."

"Anybody else?" asked Stuart.

"Dr. Saxon. That is, if he would stand still long enough for me to learn his story."

"Yes, the doctor would have to be included for sure," replied Eric. "Is that all?"

"The Salvation Army would have to be included, and that Miss Dwight," replied Andrew. "Then I would throw in some representative miners tangled up in various situations, and my book would be quite interesting; that is, if their situations weren't so difficult as to never become untangled," added Andrew frankly. "I've never written a book in my life, but Champion certainly has plenty of material for one."

"Perhaps someone will put us in a story someday," Stuart said contemplatively. "Meanwhile, my dear friends, back to our present situation. Everyone could probably write one good story if he had to, for everybody has a story to tell. And since becoming a Christian, I'm learning that every human being is a tragedy just waiting to happen or at least a possible one." Stuart spoke with such dignity that it could be called nothing less than reverential. "I see a new world, and I now understand Paul's statement, 'If anyone is in Christ, he is a new creation; old things have passed away; behold, all things have become new.' And nothing seems more new to me than human beings."

"They seem pretty old and commonplace to me sometimes," Eric said. "But I believe I know what you mean."

"Eric, I don't believe you fully understand, but I'll let you think you do. Now, we'll see if three intelligent and willing men who care for humanity can actually do anything to help solve the problems that have been thrust upon them. Why don't we look at the money issue first?"

Stuart paused, and Andrew looked thoughtfully at him. All three men were finally at a point in their discussion where they were truly focused on the problem at hand.

"Well," Eric said at last with his usual bluntness, "you're the only one with any money. It's for you to say what can be done financially."

"As nearly as I can figure," continued Stuart as if he had not heard Eric, "the property left by my father is worth in the neighborhood of four million dollars, and half of that is in the mines and their equipment. Father had total control of his property before his death and was very hands-on in operating the mines. Eric, you know how Father worked. While other mines were owned by stock-holders and run by a few large investors, Father worked from the time he was a captain in the Beury mine and basically ran the business by himself. Under his leadership it was very profitable, and today is practically in the same shape as when he left it. So under ordinary circumstances I could sell the mines for around two million dollars. Then there is nearly a million that is held in trust for Louise and, of course, is hers to do with as she chooses. The remaining million could easily be converted into cash at any time and is entirely under my control."

"Then you have a million dollars to spend?" asked Andrew simply.

"Yes, it amounts to that. Of course, the mines pay for themselves while they are running. In fact, this million represents profits and accumulated interest made by the business in less than five years."

The men fell silent again. There was a good deal of deep thinking going on within each of them. Stuart spoke first, saying, "The question we need to answer is: How can this money best be used to the glory of God? How would you use it if it were yours, Andrew?" He had asked the question suddenly, turning to the minister, who was seated with one arm resting on the table where he kept one of his favorite plants.

Andrew stared at Stuart, not knowing how to answer. Finally he exclaimed, "That's a very hard question! In my wildest dreams I would never have thought of having a million dollars to spend. I've never even made more than a thousand dollars a year in my entire life. A million dollars would buy all the greenhouses in the United States, and as for rare species of roses, it takes my breath away to imagine what this money could do. Ah, I'm off the track here, but I know what you mean. It isn't a question of what I could get for myself, but what I could get for other people. Yet I'm inclined to believe it's harder to spend money on others than on yourself."

"I don't know about that," broke in Eric. "I have always believed if I had a million dollars to spend in Champion, I could make good use of it."

"Go on, Eric, then tell us what you would do," Stuart said, turning to him.

"Well, for one thing," Eric reflected, his dark eyes glowing under the impulse of his idea, "I would build a house or hall dedicated to the cause of labor. I would see it as the center of every useful and inspiring idea that could elevate and enlarge a person's thinking, emotions, and sensibilities. It would have a platform where the best speakers, singers, and preachers could bring their messages to the people. I would use it to place two of the world's greatest joys—music and flowers—within easy reach of every workingman in Champion. All of this would be under one roof and would all be dedicated to the common people. Oh, how I've spent many sleepless nights planning how I would spend other people's money for my people!" He paused, sharing a smile that was sadder than tears.

"Oh, the heartache I've felt over wasted music and the natural perfume of God's rich earth! Yes, if I had the money, I would bring some of these things to those who spend their lives underground. Many of these people live like animals, as if God had never made birds to sing and violets to bloom. I am almost hesitant to share with the two of you what I have felt. I've seen the rich and spoiled men and women of society wasting their money by the millions on their own selfish pleasure, while thousands of children in the streets and the mines have never heard a musical note sweeter than that of an untrained voice or seen the beauty or smelled the perfume of anything better than a dusty weed by the roadside. The differences between the rich and the poor, plus the knowledge of how that money could meet the needs and bring miracles of pleasure to my brothers, along with my own helplessness to make a change in their circumstances, have nearly caused me to hate other men and nearly blaspheme God and His universe. Money!" Eric cried as he clenched his fist on his knee.

His face, pale and weary from his recent injury, glowed with the fire of an inner spiritual agony as he continued, "If only I had what will be wasted in this town this winter on foolishness and wicked behavior, I could make a thousand children happy for a lifetime. And I could save hundreds of souls from cursing God for having been born into a world of such inequality. Sometimes I feel I've already lived in hell instead of earth. But . . . please excuse me . . . I didn't mean to get off on all of this. Certainly no one knows better than I that I'm often mistaken and narrow-minded, not to mention one-sided and unreasonable. All the same, I'm sure that, as there is a God who rules and judges, there will come a day of reckoning for the men and women who have spent His money on their selfish pleasures, simply ignoring God's children who have gone through life starved and parched from the lack of the beautiful gifts of their Father that He intended for the enjoyment of all mankind."

There was silence in the room. Andrew went over to the window and looked out, but then rushed back to the table. Without saying a word, he cut half a dozen of his choicest roses from their plants, hastily rolled them up in some paper, and without a word of explanation, hurried from the room. Eric and Stuart could hear him bounding down the stairs three steps at a time. They looked at each other in total silence and then stood to look out the window.

Crossing the square through one of the diagonal paths made by the snowplow was Mrs. Binney. She was the wife of the injured miner and had been the one who had come to see Dr. Saxon the day before Stuart and Eric had been trapped in the mine. She was carrying a basket on one arm and was on her way home after having been down to Champion from her house on the hill. Andrew had been up to see her husband, Jim, several times during his recovery.

As Eric and Stuart continued to watch from the window, they saw Andrew trudge through a snowdrift nearly as deep as his neck and then stop an astonished Mrs. Binney just as she was turning to cross the railroad tracks. He gave her the bouquet of roses, which she placed in her basket. Her head looked strange, covered as it was with a shawl and a bonnet as protection from the cold, but she bowed it slightly toward Andrew, indicating her appreciation. Andrew rushed back to the hotel, darted upstairs, pulled a broom from his closet, and returned to the hallway to brush the snow from his clothing. Still panting, he said, "Excuse me for running off like that. I'm impulsive at times, but never in a dangerous way."

"Wouldn't it be wonderful if that impulsiveness were catching?" Eric said with an air of significance.

Stuart had returned to his chair and was deep in thought, mulling over a great many things. "I'm wrestling with a problem that is larger than any other that has ever challenged me," he finally said, as the others remained quiet. "I need much more wisdom and knowledge. I believe, as Eric does, that money can produce miracles of some sort in Champion. But should I simply say, 'Look at me! I'm the great Stuart Duncan—the mine owner! I have a million dollars that I'm going to spend for your benefit, my friends. How would you like for me to spend it—on libraries, soup kitchens, music, flowers, lectures, preaching, or what? I'm ready to Christianize, elevate, improve, and lift you from your difficult lives. I'm ready to bridge the great chasm that lies between the rich and the poor, and the educated and the ignorant. Just keep quiet and my million dollars will do the rest!' Is that the idea? To use a million dollars to usher in Christ's millennial kingdom? Is there really any relationship between a million dollars and a million years of paradise? It's not so easy. I can see a hall dedicated to labor. That is a possibility. And the music and the flowers and all that. Great. But there has to be more to it than that. Yet there is one thing I know for sure. I must see for myself what the needs are in Champion. I know in a general way, but I want to know in detail."

"There's one person who can tell you all about it," said Andrew.

"Who's that?"

"Miss Dwight."

Stuart flushed. From his chair he could see the front of the Salvation Army Hall. Rhena was just going in with another woman who was also a member of the Army.

"I've been told that she is already familiar with nearly every case of suffering in Champion," continued Andrew. "She's even been out on the hills as far as Cornish Town. It's a dangerous place in winter—full of deep, uncovered holes and prospectors' abandoned mining shafts. I wouldn't want to get caught out there and lose my way after dark, especially with all this snow masking those bad places."

Stuart did not answer. From the window he saw Rhena and the other woman come from the hall carrying some bundles. They crossed the street and disappeared behind the engine house, heading in the direction of the Cornish Town path.

"What did you say?" asked Stuart suddenly as he returned from his mental journey with Rhena. Andrew and Eric were sitting where they could not see what Stuart had seen.

"I said that in case you ever fall into a hole in Cornish Town, Stuart, you might as well leave the spending of your money to Eric and me," Andrew replied, smiling at Eric. "That is, leave it to us before you fall in, for chances are, no one will be prospecting around there with a rope to pull you out at this time of year."

"I beg your pardon," Stuart said seriously. "Can we return to the subject at hand? It's quite evident we cannot settle this matter in a hurry, but I'm sure that in time the Lord will lead us to do the right thing. He hasn't given us brains and caring hearts, and then left us to make complete fools of ourselves, especially when we're trying to do what is right."

They continued their discussion for some time, but came to the realization that a detailed and definitive plan would take more time to accomplish. Even Eric, who seemed rather idealistic, had to confess that it would take more time to develop a complete solution. After all, they were planning not for just a day, a month, or even one winter, but for many years to come.

Stuart finally left for home, but only after stopping at his office to leave instructions with a clerk to deliver heating fuel and food to certain families known to be in immediate need. He also left word to send for him in case any special needs arose later that evening. The miners had recently made several personal requests for help, and Stuart, in his growing eagerness to know as much as possible about the needs of the town, had determined to handle the next emergency call himself and thereby continue to satisfy his desire for the truth.

After supper that evening, Louise and Aunt Royal were discussing the coming party or "gathering," which had been scheduled for the next week. Stuart was sitting with them in the living room beside a beautiful, roaring fire. The fireplace and mantel were comprised of handsome pieces of imported marble. They had not yet turned on the lights, for it was not quite seven o'clock.

"What kind of decorations are you planning for our gathering?" asked Louise. She had great respect for Aunt Royal as an authority when it came to matters of high society or entertaining, and deferred her opinion with no debate or dispute.

"I think we'd better have Nyphetia roses in the front room and small ferns with pearl roses in the dining room. Smilax and carnations will be the proper trimming for the library, and lilies of the valley for the music room. The last reception I attended in New York, the Dupreys decorated the entire house with lilies of the valley, and the effect was lovely."

"What did you say it cost?" asked Stuart, attempting to take part in the conversation. He had heard only a part of what Aunt Royal had said. She looked at her nephew with surprise.

"I didn't say. I heard that the flowers cost about a thousand dollars, yet flowers are only one small cost for a Duprey reception."

"It must have been lovely," said Louise, clasping her hands so that her diamond rings shone conspicuously in the light from the fire.

"I think it must have been horrible," Stuart said quietly.

"Horrible?" Aunt Royal spoke as if she had not understood her nephew.

"Yes. Well, not the flowers, but the use of that much money to decorate someone's house simply for the enjoyment of people who could see lilies of the valley any time they wanted."

"Well! Well!" Aunt Royal could not get any farther.

Louise broke in with a laugh. "Oh, Stuart's been converted lately to some ideas of the communists and socialists. Didn't you know that, Aunt Royal? The next thing you know, he'll object to using roses to decorate our own house next week."

Stuart did not say anything. He was thinking of Eric's speech that afternoon, and his heart beat heavily as he thought of all the wasted music and flowers on the earth. Who was enjoying the best of these two great and beautiful gifts of God? Was it not only those who were able to pay the highest prices for them? How could it be right to squander a thousand dollars of God's own money simply to enjoy the beauty of flowers when people were suffering and dying of hunger in the nearest tenement? If it were God's money and people were only trustees of the funds, would God consider that a proper use of His money? This was only one aspect that Stuart had begun to believe when it came to the doctrine of stewardship and money.

Yet Aunt Royal was not one to remain silent, especially after someone had used the word *horrible* in connection with her decorating ideas for her social functions. She asked in a tone that was quite sharp, even for her, "Do you mean to say, Stuart, that you think we have no right to use flowers to provide enjoyment for our invited guests?"

"No, I didn't say that," replied Stuart dryly.

"What do you mean then?"

"I can't make you or Louise understand me," Stuart said after a pause.

"No, Stuart's been talking in riddles lately. He thinks we are too aristocratic and unchristian," said Louise. There was a sneer in her voice that deeply hurt Stuart.

"Why do you say that, Louise? You know I'm thinking of the poor families who are beginning to suffer right now. Surely we ought to do as much for them as for ourselves. If we spend a hundred dollars to decorate our house with flowers for a party, we ought to give twice as much to help feed the hungry. An even better idea would be to take all the money for flowers and spend it on food."

"What!" Louise angrily cried. "Spend it on the people who have caused these circumstances by their own foolishness! Who is to blame for their being hungry and cold, if not themselves?"

"The women and babies are not to blame, and they are the ones who feel the suffering the most," said Stuart quietly.

"Well, you can use your money that way if you want to, but I don't waste mine on people who don't have enough sense to know when they're well off already."

Stuart rose and stood with his back to the fire. He was moved and somewhat overwhelmed by all the new ideas that had crowded into his life since the day God had spoken to him. And he felt that the revolution taking place in him would cut squarely across all the norms of today's polite society, especially when it came to money and how to spend it.

Finally, Louise and Aunt Royal returned to the subject of the coming party, and began discussing the families who were invited. Stuart continued standing, engrossed in his own thoughts, and heard only a word now and then. Then Louise caught his attention.

"Stuart, will you sing with Una next week? You remember that duet you sang before you went abroad?"

"Yes, I'll sing if I'm here that evening," Stuart replied, with a feeling that he was quickly losing all interest in the things that he once enjoyed. He had a beautiful baritone voice that was the favorite of all his friends.

"Why, are you planning to be away?"

"No, I just don't know what might happen with the strike still going on and all."

"We've invited the Meltons and the Vasplaines. They will be very disappointed if you aren't here," said Aunt Royal.

"I'll probably be here," Stuart stated.

Louise stood suddenly and walked up to her brother. "And I invited Miss Dwight, Stuart. She refused to come, but I bet you thought I was too aristocratic to even invite her."

Stuart looked at Louise in astonishment. The words sent color to his cheeks and set his heart pounding. "You knew she would not come," he said in a low voice.

Louise seemed startled, as if she had been caught in her lie to Rhena. She went back to her seat and was silent. Oftentimes Louise enjoyed saying or doing something strange or unexpected, though her thinking was not original. She simply took malicious pleasure sometimes in startling others.

"I'm glad she refused," said Aunt Royal, who exposed her own desire for gratification and forgot diplomacy altogether. "Besides, she certainly would have felt very much out of place with us."

"Yes, that's true," Stuart said, feeling provoked into making a statement he could easily have made before his conversion. "She would have been out of place because most of your guests are un-educated boors and clowns when compared to a lady like Miss Dwight!"

Aunt Royal was speechless. She could not find anything to say at first. Then she began in her usual gentle voice, "I'm surprised, Stuart, to hear you speak that way of a common Salvation Army—"

That was as far as Aunt Royal could get. Stuart interrupted with such emotion that both women froze in astonishment, "I will not allow you or anyone else to speak one disrespectful word about the woman I love, and who, if God is good enough to me, will some-day become my wife!"

With those words Stuart walked out of the room, leaving his aunt and Louise gasping as if a pail of ice water had been thrown over them. What they said once they recovered, only God knows. But Stuart never knew or cared.

He went to his room and sat there without turning on the lights. He knew that certain things would be forever changed in his house by his brief outburst, which declared his purpose. Yet he did not regret it, although he was concerned he might have shown an unchristian spirit in his words or in how he stated them. Perhaps the "old Adam" still had a place in him? No, he said to himself, he was a new man—and the very best evidence of that was what he had just done. He knelt and prayed, however, to be forgiven if he had spoken unjustly. He was still praying when one of the house-hold servants knocked on his door, saying that he was wanted on the telephone.

A clerk in Stuart's office related that two miners had come in and were asking to see him. Stuart told the clerk to ask the men to wait. He would be there as soon as possible. He then left at once and drove into town.

The men who had come to the office were residents of Cornish Town. They had come for help, but not for themselves. It seemed that there was a miner at the farthest end of their town who was quite sick.

Stuart quickly placed a number of basic necessities in his carriage, and with one of the men riding with him to direct the way, he headed out. The night was quite dark and light snow was falling. Snowdrifts were piled high on either side of the road, and Stuart knew he could drive only part of the way. As he went by the Salvation Army Hall he stopped a minute to speak to one of the men who was standing on the steps. The hall lights were on, but no meeting was taking place.

"Miss Dwight went up to Cornish Town this afternoon with some clothes to distribute and should have been back before now. We're beginning to worry about her," the man said in answer to Stuart's question.

He drove on with a great feeling of uneasiness in his heart. He recalled Andrew's words about the abandoned pits and prospecting shafts all around Cornish Town and on the hillsides. The thought that Rhena might be in danger caused his heart to race. He drove his carriage with reckless disregard of the speed he was traveling or danger to himself. The miner who rode with him, in speaking of it later, said, "Tell you what, boys! I thought I was with the doctor, so I kept praying, like everybody does who rides with him."

When they reached the end of the road, Stuart left the horse and carriage in a shed behind one of the cottages. The people in that cottage had seen Miss Dwight come up that afternoon. She had stopped a minute to warm herself and then had left.

By the time Stuart had reached the house at the end of the miners' path, it was snowing furiously. Rhena had been there before him and had left a bundle of clothing. But that was the last anyone had seen of her. Stuart rushed from the meager cabin and down the path to the next cottage of the settlement. Yet no one had seen Rhena on her supposed return to town, and she had not passed by the two men who had gone to get Stuart. Stuart stood on the little path listening, with his heart trembling. The great pines seemed to sob under the pressure of the rising wind. Far below him the lights of Champion gleamed here and there through the falling snow.

Never had Stuart Duncan felt such love for Rhena Dwight as at that very moment. Yet he was struck with terror and choked by the fear that she might have wandered from the miners' path, fallen into a treacherous pit, and was even now lying at the bottom of one of them, dead or dying. He prayed as he stood there, "My God! My God! Save her, for I love her more than my own life!"

8

complications

Stuart had covered every inch of Cornish Town as a boy, and even now was familiar with most of its strange little lanes and paths. They seemed to crisscross the hillside like markings from some gigantic game. There was probably no other place like it in America. The old prospecting shafts were of various depths, some of them having caved in from the sides. Many of them were shaped like old cellars or cisterns with a lot of rubbish at the bottom. Others were wells, anywhere from fifty to one hundred feet deep, and especially dangerous in winter. Snow collecting on bushes growing near the shaft's mouth artfully concealed the areas of great danger.

Once Stuart calmed enough to be able to think and act, his first thought was that Rhena must have attempted to take a shortcut by way of one of the miners' paths from the upper part of the settlement of Cornish Town that headed toward Champion. In the darkness, and from confusion caused by snow making even old landmarks appear different, she must have stumbled into one of the shafts. Assuming he was right, he ran back to the house where he

knew Rhena had been, and from which he had just come, to bor-
row a lantern. He then headed out on a path, which in his previous state of mind, he had completely forgotten existed. After
following it only a short distance, the lantern revealed a small black
object in the center of the path. He stopped and eagerly picked it
up, discovering it was a lady's winter glove trimmed with fur at the
wrist. He immediately recognized it as Rhena's, for he had seen her
wearing that very kind of glove just a few days earlier. He stuffed
it in his pocket and hurried on, yet with a sense of dread and horror over what possible discoveries might lie ahead. The miner who
had ridden with him, at Stuart's suggestion, had gone to the little
settlement to get others to venture out and join in the search. So at
this point he was all alone in the mysterious shadows of the pine-
covered slope.

Every step he took over the small, barely defined trail was like a
step into an unknown land. Yet even though filled with terror from
this unusual adventure so suddenly thrust upon him, he remembered walking this same path on a warm summer day as a boy only
ten years old. The smell of the balsam trees, which emitted their
pungent aroma in the warmth of the sun, seemed to be in his senses
now. Several people had evidently traveled the path that very day,
for the snow was packed down, and their footprints were not yet
wholly covered by fresh snow.

Quite a long distance from the place where he found the glove,
Stuart came to an old stump of a giant pine of many years before.
The path made a turn around the base of the stump, and as he continued on, praying in his heart for mercy and safety to be shown to
Rhena, he saw her. She was as white as driven snow and was lying so
still that he dared not think what it might mean. She had fallen over
a clump of ore that had rolled onto the path, and one hand and arm
lay stretched out directly over one of the most dangerous pits on the
hill. How close she had come to instant and certain death!

Crying out, Stuart picked her up, not daring to ask whether what he held in his arms was dead or alive. He told himself he would not ask, but he certainly knew she was not conscious. He began to feel his way down the hillside, more by instinct than by sight or touch. For some reason he felt confident that he would not fall into any of the shafts with his burden, and with strength and purpose even greater than his usual determination he continued down the path, being sure to keep his eyes on the glimmering light from the nearest cottage. Finally, he reached the original path he had taken and turned onto it from the one where Rhena had experienced her accident. The light from the cottage had now disappeared, for he was in a hollow or depression on the slope that had occasionally been used by the miners as a crude roadway to one part of the Davis mine. As he entered the hollow, he felt, rather than saw, that tracks had recently been made there through the snow. He continued very cautiously, holding Rhena, who was still unconscious.

Suddenly, Stuart heard a sound from above him on the hillside. He stopped to listen, thinking it was the sound of sleigh bells. Feeling he could not trust his hearing, he listened more intently. Yes, it was too common a sound in Champion every winter for him to be mistaken. As he listened, he peered up the slope toward the sound. The wind was calm in the hollow, so the snow fell straight down and onto his face. Yet he finally saw a horse emerge from the opaque space like a large shadow with a vague outline of something behind it.

Stuart shouted and instantly knew there was only one man in all of Champion or DeMott, or the entire area for that matter, who would dare drive up and down the hillsides of Cornish Town or Davis Hill on such a winter night. It was Dr. Saxon, who had been to see Jim Binney and had taken the old road up the hollow to save time. It was often said in Champion that the doctor would take a shortcut through the fires of hell itself rather than go around, especially if he had a patient in great danger on the other side.

The horse was much like his master and could find his way over the hills and through the rough trails like a mountain goat. He had a special gift for plowing through snowdrifts, and one of the miners said that he once saw the doctor's horse help his master right the carriage when it tipped over by sitting on the higher end of the axle, while the doctor pushed on the other side. Certainly no lighthouse using its saving light to rescue a lost mariner has ever provided as much joy as Stuart felt upon seeing the familiar horse and carriage. The horse trudged ahead through a deep hole filled with snow and nearly stumbled over Stuart as he stood there holding his precious burden.

"Whoa! Steady there, Ajax!" cried the voice of the doctor. The carriage bounded from the hole, suddenly returning to full view like a snowplow on an engine just after plunging through a drift.

"Doctor!" Stuart cried. "Thank God! Quickly! Rhena is either dead or dying! I found her unconscious on the upper trail!" He trudged on through the snow to the side of the carriage and placed Rhena on the seat beside the astonished doctor.

"Well, well! If this doesn't beat the Salvation Army drum all to pieces! I can't escape my practice even in this Cornish Town hollow. You take the prize for furnishing work for me on the spot. Are there any more of the Army dead, wounded, or dying around here?"

"Hurry, Doctor! Save her! Is she dying? Is she seriously hurt?"

"Humph! Well, I tell you, Stuart, she's a spunky lass. Ten to one she's dangerously hurt, but, no, she's not dead." While the doctor was speaking he had been examining Rhena, never wasting one second. "We'll get her to town as quickly as possible. Jump in, Stuart, and hold on to her. I can't drive and tend to her as well."

Stuart did as he was told, and the horse lunged forward at the doctor's command. Stuart couldn't help thinking the doctor was mad to drive so fast in this dangerous area. "Please be careful, Doctor! You'll kill us all! Slow down!" He gasped as he held Rhena, breathlessly bracing himself against the back of the carriage.

"You've got your hands full. Let me do the driving," was the only satisfaction Stuart received from the doctor. And before Stuart could utter an additional word of warning, they were past the dangerous part of the hollow and at the beginning of the road that led to Champion. From that point on the two men did not speak until the doctor reined Ajax in near the front of Rhena's lodging house. He had chosen to go straight there rather than stop at a cottage along the way where the prospects of good help were quite meager. The doctor then carried Rhena to her room and left Stuart outside with the carriage. Finally, when Dr. Saxon returned, he was able to bring Stuart good news. Her unconscious state was the result of a bad fall, but he did not expect any serious or long-lasting consequences.

They were standing by the carriage talking when one of the women inside looked from the door and called to the doctor, "Oh, Doctor, will you see if Miss Dwight's glove is out there somewhere? She's lost one of them."

"Stuart, shake out that blanket," the doctor said as he held up his lantern around the sidewalk next to the carriage. "It's likely around here somewhere. Do you see it?" he asked, not noticing what Stuart was doing. Receiving no answer, he shouted back, "It's not here, ma'am! Must have dropped it along the way." The woman shut the door and the doctor said, "Get in, Stuart, and I'll take you home."

Stuart climbed into the carriage without uttering a word. As the doctor seated himself, and Ajax was about to make his usual wild plunge up the street, Stuart said, "I have Rhena's glove in my pocket, Doctor, and I'm going to keep it."

"What's that!" exclaimed the doctor. He was nearly twice

Stuart's age and had known him all his life. And Stuart did not know anyone with whom he was more comfortable in sharing his secret than the doctor. "But what's the good of one glove, Stuart?" The doctor was not quite sure Stuart wanted to tell him the full story.

"Actually, I plan on having them both," replied Stuart frankly, looking directly into the doctor's face. "Old friend, can't you see I'm in love with her, and already at the most wonderful point of my life because of it?"

Stuart spoke more loudly than he had intended, forgetting that people were on the sidewalk as they rode along. Several of the Salvation Army people had gone to Rhena's lodging house to see about her. It is not likely that anyone heard Stuart, but the doctor suddenly struck Ajax with his whip, turned the carriage around in the square, and then cut across one of the diagonal lanes. Near the stage in the square the doctor stopped as suddenly as he had started and abruptly said, "I'll wait for you."

"Wait for what?" exclaimed Stuart, astonished by the doctor.

"Well, I just thought you might want to go up on the stage and tell all of Champion that you were in love with Rhena Dwight."

Stuart laughed softly. "I'm not ashamed of it. Indeed, Doctor, I do feel like shouting it out at times," he said as the doctor started Ajax again and headed onto the main street. "It's a matter of great pride with me, yet at the same time I don't want to cheapen it by saying too much, too soon. Doctor, is this like so many other events in my life, where you will say, 'God bless you, Stuart'?"

"Yes! Yes! God bless you, Stuart! As my Cornish friends say, 'This is meant to be.' You've chosen the best and bravest woman, not to mention the one with the most character, in all of Champion, or the entire state for that matter. Well, well, I knew it all along! You and Eric think I'm so busy that I don't have time to notice anything. But I see things much faster than the two of you." There was a short pause. "If I were you, Stuart, I wouldn't keep that glove very long. That just wouldn't be right in this cold weather."

"Thank you, Doctor, I've been thinking about that," replied Stuart.

He had suddenly become very deep in thought. His life had been confronted with fresh possibilities with this new experience of love, and he was aware that it would have a bearing on all the rest of the problems that knocked at the door of his heart and mind for answers. As he told the doctor good night and entered his house, his entire being was engulfed by the most profound conviction and understanding that the direction of his life would be shaped by Rhena Dwight's response to him.

And as if realizing it for the first time, he was startled by how strong his feelings were toward her, and yet how little he knew of her feelings toward him. How could she relate to him with all the social difference between them? It was true that he had come to a point where social differences meant very little to him, but how could he really tell what she thought now that her life revolved around the Salvation Army and their ways? And then there was the issue of money. She had deliberately moved from the world of wealth and fashion where he was still an integral part. Their differences seemed like a great gulf of separation. On the other hand, he reflected, they shared one great, common bond—their Christian faith. After all, wasn't that stronger than anything else? How could different living conditions or artificial social distinctions even compare with the oneness of spirit that disciples of the Master have in common? That last thought put his heart at rest.

He did not speak to Louise or his aunt about the evening's adventure when he saw them the next morning. The statement he had made to them at dinner the previous evening regarding his feelings toward Rhena had created some hostility on their part. That hostility was not immediately expressed in words, but was evident nonetheless. Louise was angry that her attempt to deceive Rhena might, and probably would, result in nothing. Aunt Royal totally ignored the subject, but there was no mistaking her complete opposition to Stuart's feelings regarding the Army woman. To be sure, she did not understand him, but Stuart was too engrossed in his own problems and plans, not to mention absorbed in his new life, to really worry about it. Yet it showed him how completely his new life would forever conflict with the old.

Two days later Stuart, Eric, and Andrew met again to talk over matters, this time at Eric's cottage. Rhena had recovered to the point that she could do some of her work, and when Stuart stopped by to see about her, she was not in. He could not help feeling that once they had the opportunity to speak, it would be quite eventful for him. He had inherited a great deal of determination from his father, and this trait, now channeled in another direction and influenced by his spiritual awakening, burned as strongly as it had in the old Stuart. But now he would use it for another purpose. The apostle Paul was Saul—only Christianized. And the new Stuart was just as likely to make needed decisions with as much quickness as the old Stuart, only now with a better and truer perspective of the meaning of his actions.

The three men met with more serious and thoughtful deliberations than ever before. The breadth and intensity of the suffering in Champion increased with each passing day, and there was no sign of the union weakening. Winter had definitely set in, and it now looked as if the mines would stay closed for the season. Stuart remembered one winter when the owners had closed the mines for a month, simply to force up the price of ore. That was when he was a boy, but he could still remember something of the suffering it created. This present situation promised to be infinitely worse.

"Eric, you have more influence with the men than anyone in these hills. Can't you persuade the union to do something to arrive at a decision?" asked Stuart a little vaguely. He felt that he needed answers to a thousand questions, but he talked in generalities because he was preoccupied.

"What can I do? The owners are the ones who need to reach a decision. Can't you persuade them to agree to our demands and your own promise of two dollars a day?" replied Eric, who never hesitated to say what he felt, no matter how abrupt it might seem.

"Apparently, I have no influence with the other owners. You should see some of the letters I've gotten from Cleveland. The owners will not give in. This whole situation is horrible. Sometimes, Eric and Andrew, I believe people are bankrupt when it comes to having any sense. What right do a third or a fourth of the miners have to keep the rest from working just because they cannot all get the same wages?"

"They don't see it that way. To them it's a principle, based rightly or wrongly on their demand for two dollars per day. At the same time, as I said the other day, I see the strike from another point of view. I am ready to acknowledge it's a miserable way to try to get justice done. The men can never make up what they have lost by being idle this long. But, good grief, Stuart!" exclaimed Eric.

He hobbled to the window and looked out on the snow-covered hills just behind the cottage before continuing, "What other way is there if the owners refuse to listen to their appeals and arbitration? Should we submit indefinitely to starvation wages because we can't help ourselves? Of course I see it from a workingman's standpoint. Boiled down to its simplest terms, the men think it quite reasonable to ask that a business like the ore industry divide its profits more fairly. Why couldn't it make many people more comfortable instead of making a select few princely rich and 'uncomfortably' wealthy?"

"Do you believe a man can be uncomfortably wealthy?" asked Andrew with a smile, as if he believed it himself.

"You don't need to go outside this room to find one who is," answered Stuart soberly. "What good can I do, even with all my money, in a case like this? I seem to be as helpless as anyone."

"No, you're not. You can relieve a great deal of suffering. Money is very powerful when used in that way," Eric protested.

"But, Eric, isn't this the situation? We have five thousand men out on strike, and a thousand of them have been offered what they demand. Yet they have refused to accept it out of sympathy for the rest. And they will never get what they want, for I can't compel the other companies to do what I think is right. Now the men are facing starvation, or at least great suffering this winter. What should I say to them—'I have money, and I'll take care of you indefinitely, or until the money is gone'? It just seems to me that a thousand men ought to go back to work if they've been offered their own terms. What do you think, Andrew?"

"I agree with you, and regard the strike as a disaster," said Andrew. At the same time, however, the men are doing as thousands of other men have done before and will continue to do, until we have a better system of settling differences between men who labor with their brains and those who labor with their hands. Is it possible to provide any work at all for them in the meantime, so that they will not be fed as a reward for their idleness?"

"What can miners do except mine? Who can manufacture jobs in an area like this, where the entire economy revolves around one thing? Besides . . . well, go on, Eric, if you want to speak," Stuart said as he noticed Eric impatiently biting his lips and nervously clenching his fists.

"I don't know what to say!" Eric blurted out emotionally. "This whole situation is maddening. The men are right, and the men are wrong. Even if their methods of gaining justice are wrong, I believe the demand for justice itself is right. But what do you expect? In all these years, who has paid any attention to the human side of this ore-producing business? Do the men in Cleveland really care about these men and their development? Or do they simply see them as a means to dig stuff out of the ground that buys them luxuries like fine clothes and houses, travel and education, and pleasures of all kinds?

"What we are now reaping is nothing but the fruit of a great deal of the sowing of selfishness in man's great passion—money. And I ask the two of you who were raised in wealthier families than I, what will it accomplish? Isn't it true that the wage earners of the world, whether ignorant, mistaken, and wrong, or even violent at times, have committed sins less grievous, at least in relation to men of great wealth, education, and social power? I'm not saying that we are perfect and never make mistakes, or that selfishness is found only in the rich. But I do believe that we would not be struggling with this present problem if those who have made their fortunes by the toil of the miners had acted like Christian men. How many mine owners have gotten together and prayed for the wisdom to settle this matter fairly? Not one of them, except Stuart here.

"And yet, I don't believe there's a man alive who can find a solution. If there is, he should stand guilty before God for keeping silent. This much is certain: no man, nation, or form of government known to civilization is free from these differences between men of muscle and men of money. In fact, only this morning the newspapers had stories of huge strikes in five different countries: England, France, Germany, Australia, and the United States. There are more than one hundred thousand men out on strike this very minute.

"I know there is great discontent, and some may say great foolishness, on the part of labor. I'll grant you that, but the fact is, we live in an age of unrest. At the very root of the trouble lies a disregard for humanity, and man's passion to gain wealth at any cost. The love of money has wrecked empires, and it will smash our civilization unless—" Eric stopped abruptly and buried his face in his hands.

Stuart, placing his hand on Eric's shoulder, simply said, "Well, Eric, God will triumph in the end. Let's hold fast to His great truths, for they will always be proven true."

The room fell silent for a moment. Then Andrew said, "I'm sure there will be no solution to these difficulties unless it comes along spiritual lines. I believe the greatest opportunity for the cause of labor is a spiritual one. I see no possible hope for better working conditions, except an appeal to and belief in Christianity. After all, it is the only source of lasting peace between different factions of society. In reality the problem lies in getting men on both sides to act like Christians. There could be no possible clash, for instance, between the two of you, even if one of you worked for the other, because you love each other. Love for one another is, therefore, the greatest thing in the world, because it is the final and greatest equalizer of all social problems and differences."

"I believe that too," said Stuart, pacing back and forth in the little room. "I don't question the final triumph of love and right, but we're not living in Christ's perfect millennial kingdom yet. And we have our own local problems here and now."

"There's no doubt we can't ignore the suffering of women and children," said Andrew, "and a lot of suffering is beginning. One of the worst things about all of this is the way men are starting to drink. They're using what little savings they have on alcohol."

"I curse the saloons, and the hell on earth they create!" cried Eric. Stuart and Andrew were startled by his vehement outburst. "We go to our churches on Sunday and preach and pray for peace and purity, forgiveness and love, and blessings on little children; and then we turn around and vote on election day, with all the alcoholics on earth, to perpetuate a system that damns every pure desire and lofty reach of humanity. Our nation's prayers should come back into our homes and down upon our churches' altars as curses until we learn how horribly foolish and wicked we've been by not living out our prayers and voting against this devil. The saloons have done my people more harm than anything else in our civilization."

Stuart was silent. For the first time he felt the full force of Eric's passion in the matter. He remembered that the last time he and his father had voted, they had voted for the licensing of alcohol. So had nearly every church member in Champion and, of course, the forty saloon owners in town.

"Well, we can't drive the saloons out this winter. They're legalized businesses, in that they have a right to sell to those who want to buy," Stuart said sadly. "This is just one more factor in the problem. Let's face it like men and hope for better things to come. Of course, Andrew is right about not ignoring the suffering of women and children. I have an idea that may be effective, and that will require the men to work instead of receiving help while being idle. But I need some more time to work it out. Meanwhile we ought to ask the doctor and the city council what is the best and most effective way of—"

There was a knock at the door and Dr. Saxon came in. "I can stay only a moment. I heard you were here, and I wanted to tell you that we've got typhoid breaking out. It doesn't look good. I've never known typhoid to come this way in winter before, but all the streams are poisoned. Jim Binney and the Sanderses' two girls have come down with it, and Cornish Town is likely to be overrun with it. I can't get these people to follow my warnings about the drainage water around here. Now I've found that they've been drinking that poisoned water all this fall. The mines ought to furnish me, as their doctor, with a company of militiamen with orders to stand guard over these obstinate, stupid old—"

The doctor choked off the next word, but then continued, "And if they don't obey, shoot 'em on the spot and save the expenses of medical attention. I tell you, Stuart, I'm going to issue a huge bill to the company for all this work I've put in lately without pay. I'm tired of it. Been out on Davis Hill every day now for a month. Tipped over this afternoon coming down the Iron Cliff road and got two bushels of snow up my sleeves. And if there's anything I hate, it's snow up my sleeves. I'm going to quit running headlong into avalanches for these ungrateful, thankless—"

Just then a loud knock at the door interrupted the doctor. All the time he was speaking he was shaking the snow off his coat onto the stove, which hissed and sputtered as the doctor continued his vigorous, growling complaints.

"Is the doctor here?" said a voice as Eric went to the door and opened it.

"Yes. What do you want?"

"Lew Trethven has broken his leg. Fell into a prospecting hole near the upper trail of Cornish Town. He wants the doctor to come right up."

"Just listen to that, will you!" exclaimed the doctor, who was listening hard to catch every word. "Trethven has broken each leg three separate times since I've been here. If he had six legs, he'd break every one of 'em. And he always falls into a hole at the end of the day, when I'm the farthest away and feel the least like going to see him. I've mended him so often that he looks like a bamboo fishing rod."

"Say, Doctor, can you come right up?" asked the man outside as he caught a glimpse of Dr. Saxon through the opening.

"No. I haven't had anything to eat all day since breakfast. Tell Trethven to wait until morning. He must be used to breaking his legs by now. Tell him to set the fracture himself. Tell him I'm sick. Tell him—"

Eric shut the door, and the man outside walked slowly away. The doctor saw him go by the window.

"Excuse me," he muttered, "I forgot to blanket Ajax." He darted out of the room, and Stuart saw him run around the corner and stop the man. Ajax was standing near the street where the doctor had left him, and Stuart saw Dr. Saxon hurry Trethven's messenger into his carriage. The doctor climbed in, left one foot hanging out as he usually did, and hastily turned Ajax around. For a moment it was questionable whether or not the miner would remain inside the reeling, swaying carriage. Then they disappeared behind a huge snowdrift on the side of the street.

When Stuart went home that afternoon, he carried with him a burden that grew heavier as the twilight deepened. There were still many questions to be settled as to how to spend his million dollars. Humanity was full of refusals to be helped. It was the same concern Jesus had—that people would not come to Him to receive eternal life. And these saloons! He walked past a dozen on the main street. They had never thrust themselves so conspicuously into his senses before, and as he was going by one of them, a group of miners noisily burst out and scattered over the sidewalk. One or two of them noticed Stuart and seemed ashamed as they "slithered" away. He walked past the Salvation Army Hall and could not help thinking of Rhena, living her daily life in these surroundings and working with this rough, turbulent element of society. Yet a large percentage of the miners had stayed away from the saloons so far. He lingered somewhat as he passed by, hoping to catch a glimpse of Rhena. Not seeing her, he went on home.

The next few days were ones of great anxiety for Stuart. The doctor's predictions regarding the typhoid fever outbreak proved to be correct, and it swept over Cornish Town with great fury. No one could remember when such an epidemic had raged there. Stuart sent word to Chicago and had several trained nurses come up to help at his own expense. He praised God for the things that money could do in a case like this. He also relieved Dr. Saxon by hiring two assistants, and explained to the doctor that he would pay him as if the miners were still working, and that he would do so as long as they were on strike.

All this was nothing when compared to what he longed to do. He visited with the miners in their cabins and became acquainted with their rough and meager surroundings. Several times during these visits he ran into Rhena, but she was always busy working and hardly said a word. Stuart assumed she was trying to avoid him, for her manner seemed different. He vaguely wondered if she had been told that he had found her that night in the snowstorm and had carried her to safety.

All the while Stuart was also working on the problem of the idle men, and the more he thought about it, the less confident he felt in his ability to solve the difficulty. Champion was simply a mining town and had no other industry whatsoever to occupy labor. An attempt to bring a smelting plant to the area had once failed due to the high cost of fuel. And Stuart was confronted with the problem that the men were ignorant, at least from a practical standpoint, when it came to any kind of manual labor, except for their knowledge of mining.

It is, of course, unnecessary to say that he daily attempted to use his influence with the men to persuade them to agree to his terms. Yet even while he was talking and urging, he felt his own sense of great unrest. In spite of his being a mine owner, he held a certain admiration for the men who refused to come back to work in the Champion mines on his terms. He respected their reasoning when they said, "It's not right for us to take the dollars, while all the rest of the DeMott men are shut out because of the old wages offered by the other companies." The whole situation was deadlocked as far as the union was concerned.

And Stuart was facing another problem that was new to him: trying to apply the teachings of Jesus to a complicated situation of events and conditions in the business world. He was willing to act on those teachings as fast as he discovered them, but other men connected with the strike on both sides were not willing. Like it or not, he was part of the commercial, business system. And even with as much as he had done to help, he saw little relief for the men of Champion and their families. Also, he had not had enough practice in using his money for the benefit of others to know how to do it wisely or in a way that would produce permanent results.

The week went by, and it was finally the night of Aunt Royal and Louise's party. Stuart dreaded the occasion because his heart was not in it at all. To him it seemed cruel to be having a festive, expensive, and elaborate gathering at a time when little children were dying nearby. He thought of the rugged men and women in their wretched miners' cabins, tossing and turning from the scourge of the fever that knocked with its bony knuckles of death on nearly every door in Cornish Town. That messenger of death was grimly calling them one by one from the burning heat inside to its cold embrace outside.

Stuart spent the day in a round of visits and at various stops found Andrew, Rhena, and Eric. All of them were weary and sad with the burdens they had carried and all they had done. Rhena especially seemed to show the strain of her great sacrifices, and once Stuart came very close to confronting her about her overwork. If he had, however, it is doubtful he could have kept from telling her of his love for her in the same breath. Somehow he kept from telling her, and late that evening he went home with as great a heartache as he had ever known. He seemed to believe he had to spend that day in as sacrificial and helpful a way as possible, as some kind of atonement for the way he was to spend the evening.

If anyone were ever in a poor frame of mind to enjoy the festivities of high society, Stuart was that person. Jim Binney had died that afternoon, and Stuart had arrived just in time to see Rhena kneel by the bed and pray as Jim's spirit left his rugged tabernacle and returned to God who had given it. The words of the prayer, the deep sobbing of a distraught wife and mother, the cries of the children, the wretched cabin with its few broken pieces of furniture, the patches of snow on the floor, the dirty windows, and the solemn dying of humanity raced through Stuart's mind. These thoughts troubled his heart as he walked down his stairs into the beautiful rooms, decorated with their garlands and bouquets of expensive flowers. He was grieved by the perfumed refinement that wealth produces when it is so cunningly spent.

The guests arrived dressed in the latest styles and the best that money can buy, and the conversation was light and pleasant. Listening to them, a stranger could never have guessed that there was suffering anywhere in the world. The theme of the music was love, flowers, and beauty; and used sentimental phrases without meaning, or ones with a double meaning. For the first time in his life, this kind of party filled Stuart's entire being with unspeakable loathing. To him it was like a dance in a cemetery, where the dancers imagined waltzing over fragrant meadows arrayed with beautiful white blossoms, while in reality they danced on human graves, covered with the black soil of newly dug plots.

He would never know how he survived the evening. He sang with Una Vasplaine when Louise requested it, and received loud applause when they were finished. Una was beautifully dressed and was very attractive, with large, dark eyes—much like many English girls. *She's so different from Rhena,* Stuart remembered thinking to himself during the evening. He struggled greatly to even carry on a conversation, never having been skilled at the small talk that those of upper society handle so well.

He wondered how the happy and satisfied people of the world, made in the image of God, could find no better way to spend their time. They seemed to meet for hours every week dressed in their best clothes, eating expensive and indigestible food, singing songs that did not contain one noble aspiration higher than some sickly sentiment, and exchanging idiotic words thrown into sentences that had no hint of sacrifice, heroism, or humanity in them. They would sit at little tables and play cards hour after hour, and never give a moment's thought to the continual needs of suffering humanity. Then they would go home to sleep late the next day, only to prepare again for another evening of arranged flowers, card tables, menus, and decorations ad infinitum, ad nauseam; and dare to think of themselves as the best society has to offer.

Yes, the world must be running very smoothly. There must be no real suffering, no inequality, no need of heroism or self-sacrifice, and no need for speaking except to exchange empty compliments. There is no point in using time for anything other than making money or spending it, where women smile and sing, where flowers are fragrant, and where dancers' feet glide on polished floors to stringed orchestras sitting behind palm trees in lovely alcoves. After all, isn't the world society itself? Is there another world that begs for tears and groans, sacrifices and crosses, and bloody sweat and agony? Strike up the music! Play it faster and faster! Let us eat, drink, and be merry, for tomorrow we die!

Surely, upper society must be right. The Aunt Royals and Louises of the world are very proper and correct in their ideas of what constitutes the right thing to do. Surely, they are not mistaken in this matter. Yet if they are, the coming Great Judgment Day will reveal it to them. But death and judgment are two disturbing facts, and I beg upper society's pardon for even mentioning them. Strike up the music even faster and faster! Let's not think too much, for thinking leads to action, and action leads to sacrifice, and sacrifice is not agreeable to those of high society.

And so continued Stuart's thoughts throughout the evening. By eleven o'clock, however, most of the guests had gone. Aunt Royal had set the ending time at eleven out of respect for the recent death in the family. The Vasplaines had sent their coachman home and decided to walk, following the English habit of walking home for their health. They had quite frequently done this while visiting the Duncans.

"It's a beautiful night, won't you walk with us?" asked the younger Vasplaine as they stood in the hall, looking out at the snow-covered hills. It was a lovely sight in the moonlight.

"Yes, let's go, Stuart!" cried Louise.

Aunt Royal gave her consent, so before Stuart knew it, he was serving as escort to Una. It would have been quite awkward to have refused and would have been more trouble than it was worth. Hal Vasplaine walked with Louise a short distance behind.

As they reached the town square and began walking across it, they heard the Salvation Army singing a hymn. The hall was lit up, and the meeting was still going on. These words rose into the still night air:

> Yes, Jesus left His home on high,
>> Out of love, out of love;
> To suffer death for you and I,
>> Out of love, out of love.
> Our sinful sins were on Him rolled,
> Oh, look, poor sinner, and behold!
> He shed His precious blood, we're told,
>> Out of love, out of love.
>
> He had nowhere His head to lay,
>> Out of love, out of love;
> He walked the streets by night and day,
>> Out of love, out of love.
> Oh, sinner, will you now begin,
>> Take up your cross and follow Him?

complications

He's promised He will take you in,
    Out of love, out of love!

Oh, sinner, will you stop and think
    Of His love, of His love;
To have His hands and feet so torn,
    Out of love, out of love.
Oh, will you come to Him today,
And get your sins all washed away,
And walk with us the narrow way,
    Filled with love, filled with love?

The hymn was sung to the tune "What's the News?" A real critic could have criticized its grammar, meter, and literary style; nevertheless, it struck deeply into Stuart's heart like a blazing contradiction to the entire evening he had just spent with high society and its selfishness.

Just as he and Una reached the end of the diagonal lane in front of the hall, the door opened and some people came out. And as Stuart stepped onto the curb with Una by his side, radiant in all her healthful beauty, Rhena appeared in the doorway. They were only a few feet apart, and Rhena's eyes caught Stuart's for a fleeting glance and then focused on Una. Then she shut the door, and Stuart and Una silently walked past.

9

disappointment

It was nearly half a mile from the Salvation Army Hall to the Vasplaines', and later Stuart would never be able to recall what he and Una had discussed as they walked, because he was so preoccupied with Rhena. The look on her face as the door had opened revealed a deep truth to Stuart, and if Rhena had been there instead of Una during that half mile, he would have decided to determine his destiny at once.

As it was, however, Una was initially very lighthearted on their walk, but as they neared her home, she became quiet. Then suddenly, she became quite haughty and cold in her attitude. She did not know for sure, but surmised Stuart's change in demeanor had something to do with his feelings toward Rhena. Her interest was at least piqued as to why Stuart, who was her old schoolmate, was now so indifferent to her own beauty and personality that he had once seemed to enjoy. She abruptly wished him a good evening and entered her house, leaving him standing by the door somewhat awkwardly as he waited for Louise and Vasplaine.

When they finally arrived, Stuart quickly descended the stairs, and without waiting for Vasplaine to say good night, he said, "Louise, we had better be going back. Good night, Vasplaine."

"Good night, Mr. Duncan. Good night, Louise," replied the young man as he ran up the stairs and entered the house.

For a few minutes, the two of them walked, and neither said anything. Then Stuart asked abruptly, "How long has Vasplaine been calling you 'Louise'?"

"Ever since we were children," replied Louise in a mocking tone. She seemed quite animated and never looked so pretty in all her life.

"But he's never said it in that tone of voice," replied Stuart. He looked at the face in the fur-trimmed hat.

Louise looked back at Stuart with just the faintest indication of a sneer on her lips. "Hal asked me to marry him," she said at last.

"And what did you tell him?" asked Stuart quietly.

"I told him I would."

The two walked on in silence that was broken only by the crisp sound of the dry snow under their feet.

"But do you love him, Louise?" Stuart asked gently.

"Oh, I like him well enough. He is—"

"Stop, Louise! I can't bear to hear you talk like this about such a serious matter. Do you even know what sort of a man Vasplaine is?"

Louise became irate in a flash. She wrenched her arm from Stuart's and spoke with deep emotion in her voice, "No! Do you think I spy on him to learn his habits? He's like most other young men, I suppose. What difference does it make? What right have you to pass judgment on him?"

Stuart was stunned at first by her reaction. Then he recovered and replied, "Louise, I love you. You are my sister. I say this only because of what I know, and I'm telling you that if you marry Hal Vasplaine, you will be miserable. Louise, listen to me!" Stuart continued, for the moment forgetting his own concerns due to his love for his sister. "This man who has asked you to marry him is . . . Oh, Louise, he will wreck your life! He is—"

"Please don't say any more," interrupted Louise coldly. "I have promised to marry him. I like him. I believe I may even love him, since you've so brutally attacked him behind his back. You want to claim the privilege of marrying beneath you. So let me do the same, if that's what you call it."

Stuart reeled almost as if he had been struck. He had been standing facing Louise since she took her arm from his. He ran his hand across his eyes, and then in a low voice, he said, "Let's go home. We will never understand each other."

Without a word Louise took his arm again, and they walked on in total silence. By the time they reached the town square most of the lights were off, except in the houses where the sick and dying lay. Everything was wrapped in the quiet of a still winter night. The Salvation Army Hall looked cold and bleak, its unpainted siding black with age. Yet there was a light shining from Rhena's boarding-house room, which they also passed along the way. Stuart trembled as he walked by, fearing Louise might say something. She did not. In fact, neither spoke a word until they reached home.

Aunt Royal was still up and waiting for them. "You must have walked fast," she said, looking intently at them both.

"We did," replied Stuart. "It's a very cold night."

He went into the library, where a fire was still burning. Even that room was still heavy with the sweet aroma of roses and carnations. After Louise shared a few words with her aunt, they followed Stuart into the room, and Aunt Royal seemed as excited about something as she ever allowed herself to become.

"Louise tells me you object to her marrying young Hal Vasplaine," she said, confronting Stuart abruptly.

Stuart was surprised, for he had not expected Louise to mention the matter to their aunt. But Louise was quite angry, and impetuous natures like hers are never satisfied to wait very long before expressing resentment. Besides, it was a very natural thing for her to immediately confide in her aunt, for she could be sure of her complete agreement in this instance.

"Yes, I do object," replied Stuart firmly, looking directly into his aunt's face.

"On what grounds?"

"The character of the man," answered Stuart quietly.

"His character! Don't you know that the Vasplaines have held the loftiest places in elite society for several generations? And hasn't Hal Vasplaine been received everywhere in high society that Louise or you have been?"

"It is possible for society to have more regard for wealth and a family name than it does for strong character and godly morals. I've known this to be the case," Stuart said with a sad smile.

"Why did you allow the Vasplaines to come into the house then if they are such dreadful people?" asked Louise. She sat down in one of the overstuffed easy chairs with her feet outstretched toward the fire.

Stuart did not reply. He was distracted by the other events of the evening. And he had come to realize that his home life was now being affected by his new ideas and purposes, many of which conflicted with those of Aunt Royal and Louise. In fact, from this point forward it was certain that their lives would be the direct opposite of his. He felt that continuing the present discussion was pointless, and he longed to escape from it.

Louise, however, had no intention of letting Stuart go without first dealing a blow that she was so skilled at inflicting. "Aunt Royal, I told Stuart he should not object to my choice if I didn't object to his. I don't think, however, that we will be disgraced by a Salvation Army alliance in the family. By the way, Miss Dwight encountered Una and her escort this evening, and by the look on her face it was easy to see she thought them to be a very attractive couple."

Stuart tightly clenched his fists as he stood with his back to the fireplace. His old irate temper almost swelled to its breaking point, and nothing but the grace of God kept it from exploding. In the past his torrential temper had more than once terrified Louise, especially since she was so reckless in provoking it.

There was a deep silence in the heavily perfumed room. Stuart drew a long breath. Then he looked fearlessly into Aunt Royal's eyes, but quickly turned to face his sister.

"Louise," he said with a calm, even loving, voice, "you don't realize how much you hurt me. I plan to ask Rhena Dwight to be my wife, but I will never subject her to the humiliation of living under the roof of a house where—"

He stopped abruptly and walked out of the room, for he felt unable to finish calmly. Aunt Royal and Louise sat up quite late to discuss the matter. The whole situation was becoming unbearable as far as Stuart was concerned, and the two women agreed.

"What if Stuart marries her and brings her home?" Aunt Royal said.

"Then I will leave the house, but I don't believe Rhena Dwight will ever marry him," Louise replied.

It was there that the matter rested for the time being, at least in the minds of the two women. The next morning Stuart did not show for breakfast. He left word that he had important business at the office and could not wait for the late-morning breakfast that was so typical of Aunt Royal and Louise.

Stuart had come to the point that he felt compelled to tell Rhena of his feelings. What Louise had said about their chance encounter in front of the Army Hall greatly disturbed him, so his greatest need was to know the truth of Rhena's thoughts.

He spent the entire morning at his office where there was plenty to do. Typhoid and the needs of the miners' families had become grim realities all around Champion. The other ranges of hills were quickly feeling the effects of the double scourge of sickness and suffering as well. Scores of the miners' children were dying daily. To meet the emergency, Stuart used his money lavishly, buying everything from medicines to nursing supplies in large quantities. Spending his money in this way brought him mixed feelings. At least he was relieving some pain and anguish. It seemed like only a drop in a great ocean of misery, but he had some satisfaction in contributing in that seemingly small way.

Shortly after noon he received word that the child in the cabin at the far end of Cornish Town was dying. Stuart had no more reason for going to that particular cabin than any other where children were dying, except that somehow he felt drawn in that direction. Around two o'clock he drove up the narrow wagon road and left his horse and carriage at the same place where he had stopped the night he had found Rhena in the snow.

He walked up the path over the trodden-down snow, thinking of that night. The air was crisp and the sky clear. The whole town lay behind him in its setting of snow-draped hills. The scene was as beautiful as a picture painted by one of the masters, and offered no outward sign of the anguish and sorrow being suffered in the homes of the miners below.

He knocked gently at the cabin door, and Rhena opened it. She flushed faintly at the sight of him, but without hesitation motioned for him to enter.

The doctor was kneeling by the bed. The child was a little girl only ten years old—and she was dying. Stuart stood by the end of the plain iron bed, while Rhena sat next to the doctor. The child's father had been injured in an accident and was in bed in the next room, but her mother was kneeling by the side of the doctor.

"Is she . . . Is she going now, Doctor? Please say no. She's too young to leave us!" cried the mother as she leaned over the bed and looked into the small face.

"Yes, she's going. Soon her suffering will be over," replied the doctor very gently. No one was ever more gentle than Dr. Saxon in the presence of life's last enemy. He never relaxed his efforts until the last second of life. He looked death in the face with a frown, for that was part of his rough, abrupt character. Yet he faced the dying and those who mourned with the look of a compassionate angel.

The end was coming very quickly now, and the child's father cried out from the other room that he wanted to see his little girl once more. Stuart offered to bring him in. The doctor nodded, and Stuart walked to the man's bed, where with Rhena's help they succeeded in moving him. Then they propped him up in a chair so he could see his child. Huge tears rolled down his rough, coarse face as he sat there. Soon the doctor, holding the child's slender wrist, motioned to the father. He fully opened his wet eyes to see his daughter's faint smile. It crossed her face like sunlight crosses a meadow on a day when beautiful fluffy clouds are quickly blown by a warm breeze. As quickly as it came, it was gone, and the gray shadow of death followed closely behind. Her small body stiffened, she quietly sighed, then sighed again, and the end arrived. The doctor laid her little hand down and said, "She is gone." He turned his face away from the mother, and Stuart was startled by his expression. It was as if Dr. Saxon had seen Death, which he continually fought, and was enraged at the victory it had won over his human skill.

But then he quickly turned to console the child's mother, who had thrown herself across the bed with loud cries and screams—something that had lately become a common scene among miners' wives with the fever running rampant throughout the town. He gently lifted her up, and then half carried and half dragged her into the next room and laid her down sobbing and groaning on an old couch there. Stuart believed the doctor's face at that moment reflected more beauty, mercy, and blessing than any mortal man could ever show. When he returned, he pulled the sheet across the sweet but lifeless form, and then left the cabin. During those days, sleep and rest had become strangers to the doctor, and he never fully recovered from the terrible strain of that winter.

Rhena stayed a little while longer, doing what she could, while Stuart sent a nearby neighbor's son for the undertaker. He then promised the father he would do everything in his power to help. Rhena and Stuart left together, and they were soon walking together over the very trail where Stuart had discovered Rhena the night of her fall. She had other houses to visit in Cornish Town and needed to save time by taking the shortcut of the upper trail.

Stuart had not asked if he could go with her, but she neither assented to his company nor rejected it. He had forgotten all about his horse and carriage on the other path. Rhena seemed pensive and sad. The scene they had just witnessed deeply affected them both. Although death had become a common sight to them lately, it never lost its majesty for Stuart, and Rhena was never more moved than in the presence of that great enemy.

On most of the trail there was hardly room for the two of them, so Stuart walked behind Rhena. They were silent except to inquire of each other about different people who were sick. They were silent, that is, until they reached the big stump in the middle of the trail, next to where Stuart had found Rhena lying in the snow.

Just as she was about to walk around the old landmark, Stuart spoke to her. He was very pale and trembling. Stuart felt as if he had reached a crisis point, but once he had spoken his first words, he gained better control of himself.

"Miss Dwight, I wish to tell you something. Will you allow me to say what I have longed to say for some time?"

Rhena looked startled and her lip began to tremble. She seemed unable to answer.

Stuart continued. Now that he had made up his mind, he had his father's iron determination. Nothing would deter him from the purpose that seemed to possess and drive him.

"I have loved you almost from the first moment I saw you. Surely, you must have known, for I am a poor actor. I've not been able to conceal it, and I've not really desired to do so. My life has been transformed by this, and I have reached the point where I can no longer be silent. I know that I love you with the proper love that a man has for a woman when he is ready to ask her, with complete reverence and joy, to become his wife."

He had finally spoken, but it was not at all what he had thought he might have said. And he was unprepared for Rhena's reaction to his words.

She was dressed as usual in her Salvation Army uniform. The face in the Army blue bonnet, with its plain ribbons, was typical of an Army face seen everywhere. Yet the entire time they conversed, he felt, with a certain bewilderment, that she was no longer the Salvation Army girl standing before him. She seemed to be the society woman, Miss Rhena Dwight, daughter of Allen Dwight, the New York millionaire. In another way she was also removed from him by the very circumstances of her connection to the Army. Rhena was very pale as she spoke.

"Mr. Duncan," she said as she leaned back with one hand on the stump as if for support, "how can you say all this, after what I saw last night? After—"

"What!" cried Stuart with color rushing to his face. "Do you mean your seeing me with Una Vasplaine? We are old friends. We grew up together. I was simply walking her home after a social gathering at my house. She is nothing to me but a casual acquaintance."

"But I've been told that you were engaged," said Rhena after a slight pause.

"Who told you that?" cried Stuart impulsively, stepping closer to Rhena.

"Your sister!" Rhena spoke calmly, looking straight at Stuart, but she was still very pale.

"Louise! She lied to you. It's not true. I've never had a thought of a relationship with Una Vasplaine, except that of a friend—an old acquaintance. Don't you believe me?" Stuart spoke directly, obviously waiting for an answer.

"Yes, I believe you," said Rhena quietly.

Stuart's heart leaped at her answer.

"Then you believe me when I say I love you? You—"

"Yes, I believe you. I think you are an honest man, but what you ask is impossible."

Stuart controlled himself, and he believed whatever crisis now faced him, he must maintain that control. He began to realize that perhaps he had not yet won the love of this unusually strong and beautiful woman, as he may have assumed.

"Why impossible?" he asked with gentleness and calmness that surprised even himself.

"We live in different worlds," replied Rhena with a calmness that was just as surprising to her. "I have forever purposely separated myself from the life I once lived, and I have no desire to reenter it. I've chosen my life's work, and it is totally different from that of the elite of society and the world of which you are a part. To go back to your world would be to become a traitor to all my dearest and deepest convictions. It is impossible for me to become what I once was."

Stuart did not immediately reply. He glanced across the valley beyond the town to his own house. He could see it on the slope of the hill, palatial in its style and size.

"But I'm not really in that world anymore. The cause of humanity has become my cause. Will you condemn me to separation from you because of what I am outwardly? I loathe the selfishness and heartlessness of high society as deeply as you do. I would give anything to change who I am at this moment. If it is simply that which keeps you from—"

He could not finish. It was significant to her that he had not ventured to ask her if she loved him, and that he had not called her by her first name. He was a man of rare purpose and power in the crisis he now faced, and he would not yet expect what was perhaps still unavailable for her to give. She was moved deeply, and when she spoke again, Stuart had his first glimmer of hope.

"I believe you see the cause of humanity as I see it, Mr. Duncan. I have believed it since that night in the Army Hall when you told me the story of your conversion. It was so similar to my own experience that I was startled by it. After going home from a festive party a few years ago, I was awakened by a voice. I saw and heard a divine messenger, and when I left my father's house the next day, I left as an outcast from my family and friends. And I have never regretted it. But even with this common experience, there is a great gulf between us. If I were to become your wife," Rhena said the word with some difficulty, "it would be at the expense of the life of service I have chosen. It would be—"

She stopped as if afraid to trust her own voice. Stuart did not take advantage of her emotion to look at her. He continued gazing down the valley.

"Isn't our Christian faith enough of a common basis for us to do a common work together? Can't we accomplish more together than we ever could alone?" he asked. Although his heart hungered for her love, he knew he could not take what she did not have to give.

Rhena answered quietly, "I just can't. And I feel unable to even thank you for the greatest honor a man can give a woman because I am not worthy of it."

"No!" Stuart cried at last, turning to her. "I love you. Allow me to say it even if it may be the last time." Then he did what he had not initially thought of doing. But he felt there was still the possibility of an answering love in this woman, and his longing for her would not permit him to walk away without fully exposing his heart.

Stuart took Rhena's glove from his pocket, and as he showed it to her, he cried, "You see! I was walking along this very path one night—a night of great beauty to me. I found you lying over there near the opening of that pit, and I picked you up and carried you to safety. And for those moments you were mine in my heart, and you were unable to say no." His voice broke, and he began to sob with great emotion, something he had never done before.

Rhena took a deep breath, standing there pale and still. "They told me Dr. Saxon brought me in. Why didn't they tell me the truth? Why didn't he tell me? I owe you my life?"

It was both a question and a statement. Stuart would not yet allow himself to anticipate the love that might become his. He stood there silently, facing her after her outburst of surprise. Finally, he gently said, "I would like to keep the glove. May I?"

She did not answer him, and he slid the glove back in his pocket. She was even more pale.

He ventured one more question, "Do you believe I love you?"

"Yes, I believe it," she answered in a very soft voice.

"I will always love you," he said. He took off his hat as an act of reverence. "Someday, once I have won your love, as I know I have not yet done, we will speak again," he added slowly. And then he turned and walked down the trail, never once looking back.

When he disappeared behind a clump of fir trees, Rhena knelt by the old stump and laid her head upon it. Her prayer was very much like the prayer the night that Louise had called on her. After some time she stood and walked down the trail, but she was not the same woman. Her heart was shaken for the first time in her life by the love of a wonderfully good man. She thought to herself, *If only he had called me Rhena, I would have called him Stuart, and it's entirely possible I might have given him everything.* It was dangerous for her to think of him. She had feelings she had never had before. And then the glove . . . Just thinking of owing her safety to him caused her to tremble. Her emotions were running wild, and if Stuart had come back at that moment, she would have said to him, "I love you! Let's spend our lives together!" As she walked to the next cottage, there was a look in her eyes that was new to them, and an emotion in her heart that would not be suppressed.

Stuart had returned to Champion, but not with a feeling of defeat or discouragement. Yes, it had become a crisis to him, but at least he had finally shared his feelings with Rhena. He regretted nothing he had said, and in spite of the fact that she had said no, something inside told him it was not final. He would certainly be the last person in the world to ever try to persuade the woman he loved into loving him in return or to beg for her love. He told himself the time would come, although he had no idea when or how, that they would belong to each other. With that wonderful thought burning within him, he began what was to be one of the busiest and most significant weeks of his life.

On Sunday of that week he joined the church. Two weeks earlier he had met with Andrew and shared the experience of his conversion to Christ. To Stuart, it seemed necessary and the most appropriate thing in the world to openly and boldly identify himself with other Christians in the organization that Christ ordained and loves. There was not a moment's hesitation in his mind about the responsibility and privilege of church membership. So it was a memorable day in his life when Andrew asked him to stand before the congregation and confirm the church covenant.

The news that Stuart Duncan was going to join the church was interesting enough to the population of Champion that it drew a large crowd. Andrew had never seen such a large congregation at St. John's. It was filled primarily with the miners and their families. Stuart was the only person received into membership at this Communion service, and when he stood at Andrew's invitation, his face was calm and radiant. It was a beautiful sight to see the two men facing each other.

When Stuart knelt to be baptized, Andrew's voice trembled for a second over the words, "I baptize you, Stuart, my brother, disciple of Jesus," and many an eye in the audience moistened. When the bread was passed, Stuart received it from one of the miners who had worked in the Champion mines ever since Stuart was a boy. He was a deacon in St. John's, and Stuart never forgot the look on the old man's face as he handed the plate to Stuart, who was seated at the end of the pew. More than half of St. John's membership were Cornish, and this was a day long remembered by each of them.

As Stuart partook of the Communion elements for the first time, he saw the prospects for fellowship with these men, nearly all of whom had been employed by his father. It was true that they were what some would deem to be crude and uneducated, and that their brand of Christianity might not be very lofty. Also, at this very moment they were engaged in a struggle against management, which was contrary to Stuart's deepest convictions. Yet he had come to the point where he looked at the struggle from a different perspective. The men of the church were for the most part prayerful, honest, and above all, generous with what they possessed. Stuart did not know it, but Deacon Sam Penryck, who had passed him the bread and wine, had that very morning given one of the suffering families in Cornish Town a third of his own savings. He had saved the money in an effort to help his own family survive the strike that winter.

It was not the differences between them that Stuart was considering as he sat there, but the relationship he might have with them as a new member in the body of Christ. Every day that passed since his father's death, he was growing more and more to believe that he was indeed his brother's keeper, and even more so since his conversion and today's Communion service. In fact, Andrew's prayer for Stuart touched on that very issue, and the service overall made quite an impression on him.

Before the close of the service, Stuart asked Andrew if he could say a few words. He then very simply, yet profoundly, shared his Christian faith, and he asked for the prayers of the people that God might grant him strength and wisdom to live the true life of a disciple. The people were deeply touched by the strength and power of his words, especially coming from such a young man. They did not show their emotion outwardly at the time, but they felt it nevertheless, and they talked about his words on their way home that day. They had not seen anything quite like this in Champion during their lifetimes.

In spite of this and the tremendous influence that Stuart was gaining with the men, the union continued to hold out for the original terms and showed no signs of weakening. The Salvation Army continued to exercise a restraining influence over a majority of the miners, although drinking was increasing. About the only hope Stuart had for a settlement was that the Cleveland owners would be compelled to concede before the winter was over. After all, the demand for ore had increased over the last few weeks. Yet he little expected that the full wage demanded by the miners would be granted even then, and he knew from past history that very few large strikes were ever successful. But he hoped that the owners and union might find some middle ground on which to stand, so the miners could go back to work.

The remainder of the week after the Communion Sunday would also prove to be memorable for the people of Champion, especially for Stuart. The terrible epidemic had seemed to reach its peak, with most of its victims being children. The number of deaths each day was appalling. Andrew, Eric, Dr. Saxon, Rhena, Stuart, nurses, and all the available help from the Christian community in town were battling the enemy with all that their might, skill, attention, and money could muster.

Stuart and Rhena crossed paths several times that week, usually at the bedside of a dead or dying child. They said very little to each other, for each seemed to be waiting for something. Rhena was thin and tired, yet there was a new look in her eyes that she dared not let Stuart see.

As if the epidemic were not enough, the winter was also taking its toll on the hearts of the people. Never had Champion seen such huge snowdrifts or such severe cold. Each night bitter winds would sweep down the hills, and once the evening train had plowed its way out of the station on its dreary trip westward, Champion seemed to be abandoned by God and man. All connection to the rest of the world seemed cut off, the surrounding iron hills seemed to press down upon the town, and the long, terrible night began. Each one was a night of agony for those who died as well as for those who lived. The date of the huge strike and the terrible epidemic would forever be etched into the minds of the children who would be fortunate enough to be left untouched by the grim finger of death.

One night that week Stuart came home very late. He was thoroughly exhausted, chilled down to his bones, and numb from the huge weight of his responsibilities. His heart was crying out to God, "O Lord! How long! How long!" He went straight to his room and sank into a deep sleep. Then between two and three in the morning he awakened with the feeling that something was wrong. The feeling was so strong that he got up, dressed, and went to the window overlooking the town. The cold night air was among the most bitter ever known, and the wind was blowing like an icy gale across the valley. Even the Duncan mansion, which was warmed with the best and most expensive heating equipment, felt the shock of the cold that cut its way through everything.

Suddenly, Stuart saw a light at the lower end of Cornish Town. The miners' houses or cabins there were built for the most part of logs or planks of wood from the mill. They were crowded very closely together at the lower part of the town. As he watched, the light jumped higher, and his heart began pounding as he realized that one of the cabins was on fire. The horror of a fire on such a bitterly cold night stopped him in his tracks, but only for a second. The next instant he was downstairs, had thrown on his overcoat, and was out of the house and speeding down the road.

As he reached the square, lights were beginning to come on in windows all around. An alarm had sounded and people were rising from their beds. By the time he reached Cornish Town, half a dozen houses were blazing. The miners had turned out en masse and were fighting the fire like fiends, but the intense cold, the high wind, and the closeness of the cabins to one another on that side of the settlement made the fight incredibly hopeless.

Stuart ordered all the sick and elderly to be carried out of the houses that were closest to the fire, and he worked like ten men. There was no water available, although the engine and hose companies had made a desperate effort to reach the settlement. The tremendous snowdrifts and the condition of the roads made it impossible. The snow itself was the only weapon within reach. It was piled onto the lower-roofed cabins by the excited miners, who saved some houses around the edges of the fire by using this novel method. But everything in the direction of the wind was consumed, and finally the men placed all their efforts on rescuing the people.

As Stuart was beginning to help someone carry a dying child from a cabin, a large blazing timber was flung by the furious wind, as if thrown by a giant hand. It flew directly over the couch where the child was lying and struck Stuart. It knocked him off his feet, causing the man who was helping with the child at the other end of the couch to also stagger with his burden and fall. Stuart did not get up. At that moment Dr. Saxon came out of the adjoining cabin, and the man who had been helping Stuart stood to his feet and yelled for the doctor. Saxon hurried over, picked Stuart up as if he were a little boy, and carried him down the path to Eric's cottage. In recounting the story later, the miners said that Dr. Saxon's face, as it reflected the light of that horrible fire, was the face of a man who looked both death and hell in the eyes, and dared them to even try to take his beloved friend away.

Fortunately, Eric's cottage was not in the direct line of wind and fire that night. The doctor laid Stuart down, and as he did so, a woman rushed into the cottage and threw herself down next to his body. It was Rhena, and she cried out as she knelt there, "Stuart! Stuart! Can you recognize me? I love you! Oh, Doctor, he's not dead is he? Tell me he's not. Oh, how I love him! I love him!"

"At this rate," said Dr. Saxon grimly, "we'll have to build another stage in the town square!" But then he looked at Stuart as he lay there, deaf to all those words of love from the woman whose heart was finally his. The doctor's face looked very grave and concerned.

10

friendly
debate

Two weeks after the fire and accident, Stuart was still at Eric's cottage, and Eric sat by his bed. Stuart's injuries were so serious that no thought of moving him was ever considered. During some anxious days and nights, Eric had hardly left his side. Andrew had begged to be allowed to sit with Stuart, but Eric had insisted upon doing it himself, refusing to give way to anyone else.

Yet there was one other who wanted to sit with Stuart even more than Andrew, and who jealously regarded Eric's actions. That person was Rhena, who would often slip into the cottage when the doctor would visit. She would sit dry eyed and pale, with her heart's hunger for love staring out of her eyes that burned over Stuart. It was as if she thought the very force of her compelling affection would awaken him to consciousness and full life again. No longer did Rhena try to hide her feelings toward Stuart. The doctor came in quietly one day while Eric, who was exhausted by his long vigil, was sitting asleep at the side of Stuart's bed. The doctor also found Rhena there, but on her knees praying. The intensity of her desire for Stuart's recovery showed itself in her audible petition to God.

"O Lord, my God, save him! What has he done that he should die? Oh, how can I say, 'Thy will be done'? I never loved him before. Spare him, God of all goodness! He is greatly needed in Your kingdom here on earth! Surely, there are others who would be less . . . Oh, dear God, what am I saying! But he is my love! And he does not know that I love him!"

"I beg your pardon!" interrupted the doctor. "But you're mistaken about that. He knows it perfectly well. Just tell him four or five times more if you think it's necessary."

Rhena turned her head toward Stuart. He lay there with his eyes open for the first time in days. He was completely conscious and had a smile on his face that was heaven to her. She turned on her knees, bowed her head over Stuart's hand, and put her lips on it. Then to the doctor's surprise, she fell over and fainted.

"It never ceases to amaze me the things that women can think of to do to surprise a man!" said the doctor. He picked Rhena up and carried her over to a couch at the other end of the room.

Eric was startled from his brief nap, while Stuart had shut his eyes again. He had lapsed into his former state of unconsciousness, but with a smile still on his lips.

"If any lass has a right to faint, this one has," stated the doctor flatly. "Are you going to tumble down again, ma'am?" he asked as Rhena began to come to. "You can if you want to. Do you want to cry? Come now! That's a good girl! Cry a little. It'll do us all some good. Want a handkerchief? Here's mine."

Rhena sat up suddenly, grabbing Dr. Saxon's hand. "Oh, Doctor, he will get well, won't he? Is he better? There is hope, isn't there? He knew me for a moment! You do believe my prayer will be answered?" Rhena was crying softly, for she was weary and nervous from the great stress and strain of the last two weeks.

"I've heard worse prayers get answered," replied the doctor abruptly.

"But do you think . . . Oh, Doctor, it will be the death of me to think of . . . Tell me, what do you think? Is he . . . Will he live?"

The doctor shut his lips tightly. Rhena watched him with her hands clenched over his. She did not realize it, but the tight grip of her slim fingers hurt even the doctor's rugged, knotty fists. Finally, he answered her. "I think . . . Yes, I am quite sure, now that he knows that you care for him a little, he has a fighting chance."

"Care for him a little!" replied Rhena with a smile that melted the doctor completely. "Doctor, were you ever in love?"

"No," replied the doctor. "But if I were, I'd have to put up still another stage in the town square. One apiece wouldn't be too much for three fools like Stuart, you, and me."

"What's this nonsense he's talking, Rhena?" asked Eric, coming over to the end of the room where they were.

"It's not nonsense," said Rhena with more color in her face since the day Stuart had first spoken to her. She went over to the side of Stuart's bed and sat down there to watch him. She had great hope now. The doctor had told the truth, for it was indeed love that finally brought Stuart through the ordeal and on to recovery.

"I've heard that people who were in love could live on nothing," the doctor said, "but I do believe if Stuart hadn't regained consciousness long enough to hear your little prayer, I'd have had two funerals on my hands pretty quickly. Well, I've never understood you women. There you were one minute as limp as a dead fish, and the next minute as lively as a Salvation Army tambourine. If I could get this product they call love bottled up in a prescription and dole it out in severe cases, I believe it would do more good than all the bacteria killers on earth."

They all shared some wonderful days once Stuart was declared to be out of danger. Andrew celebrated by bringing over his choicest blossoms. He arranged two vases of roses on a table where Stuart could see them, and laid a beautiful white carnation on the bed within reach of Stuart's fingers.

"It's the only one I've been able to get this winter, Stuart. Isn't it a beauty? It's a new variety. Do you know what I've named it? I took the liberty of calling it the 'Rhena Dwight.'"

When Rhena came in a few minutes later, Andrew and Eric pretended to be busily talking at the other end of the room. Stuart picked up the carnation and spoke feebly, but the light of life was in his eyes. "This flower is called the 'Rhena Dwight.' At least, that's what Andrew says. Will you take it because of the love I have for you?"

Rhena took the flower and kissed it. Then she shyly placed the blossom against Stuart's lips. She then returned it to his hand.

"No," she said, "you keep the 'Rhena Dwight' for the love I have for you."

Is it any wonder that Stuart got well very quickly after that? In fact, one week later he was almost recovered. He was able to take part in meetings regarding the strike that seemed to force themselves into Stuart's bedroom at Eric's, in spite of what Eric tried to do to prevent it. The previous three weeks, which were a total blank to Stuart, had been full of horror and misery for the miners across all the ranges of hills. The fire that dreadful night had made three to four hundred people homeless. The deaths from typhoid had lessened some in Champion, but at DeMott the daily mortality had increased. Most of the suffering came from the lack of clothing, heating fuel, and food. The winter had continued with terrible severity, yet the union held out with remarkable stubbornness, even though it had long since depleted its fund that helped its members financially. The week that Stuart had regained consciousness, however, there was a rumor a break would come very soon.

Stuart returned to his full strength and renewed vitality, ready again to tackle the labor dispute, especially after realizing what the last three weeks had added to the suffering of the people. He was radiant with the love of Rhena, now completely his. He recognized she particularly loved him for his desire to ease human suffering, especially as it touched both of their lives in Champion. He now set himself to the task ahead, but with the added warmth and enthusiasm of her godly wisdom. And he was not alone in wanting Rhena included when Eric and Andrew came to discuss important matters. The others had learned that a woman's wisdom often supplies the necessary solution to bring practical relief to a situation. So Rhena became an indispensable partner with them in their meetings and discussions.

"Something needs to be done soon for the people who lost everything in the fire," said Andrew. The little group of four were in Eric's room, with Andrew seated in a chair, Stuart on the couch, Rhena sitting next to him, and Eric pacing the room, his dark eyes restless and burning.

"I understand they've all been comfortably cared for. But I don't see what Champion people have been able to do in the way of housing for them," said Stuart. He looked at Andrew, upon whom a great deal of the relief work had fallen during Stuart's time of unconsciousness.

"Heaven only knows how all of them have been cared for. The Salvation Army Hall has been turned into barracks, and Miss Rhena here knows how much the Army has done."

"It has done very little in comparison with what it would like to do," said Rhena sadly.

"Do you know what it would like to do?" asked Stuart, who was only just beginning to comprehend how great and pressing was the need since the fire and three more weeks of the strike.

"I'm afraid it's not much use for me to say," answered Rhena with added sadness.

"Are you forgetting my money?" Stuart responded. "What's it

186

for anyway? Why haven't you been spending it while I've been sick?" he asked almost fiercely, turning to Eric, who was still pacing the room, but had not yet spoken.

"I've spent plenty of other people's money, in my mind," answered Eric as bitterly as he'd ever spoken. "But I never spent it in reality, and when it comes to the suffering we're facing now, I wouldn't know where to stop. What right do people have to go on wasting God's property so wickedly while there is so much suffering?"

He looked at Andrew as he spoke, and Andrew, who seldom made a retort of any kind, replied, "Ask the devil. He knows more about it than I do."

"And then there is the church," continued Eric, who was irritable and nervous. Watching Stuart for so long had finally taken its toll on him. "What is the church doing in comparison with what it ought to do? Stuart, you asked me quite a while ago why I joined the Salvation Army. I'll tell you why. There was nowhere else I could go for the true expression of religion in my life. St. John's Church is a curious mixture of workingmen and tradesmen, not to mention its aristocracy. I'm sorry to have to say this, but certainly before Andrew came here, their entire purpose seemed to be to meet together in order to provide the people with nothing but good feelings and emotions. They never accomplished anything of a practical nature in helping to relieve the pressure of the physical needs of people. Everything seemed to evaporate into feelings, hymn singing, and prayers that never seemed to make any difference beyond the walls of the church itself.

"I don't mean to be tearing down the Christian lives of the church members, for there are hundreds of them better than I am. But the outward expression of their Christianity through the church structure seems worthless. One person may be as strong as another, but if one of them is using a dull ax to cut down a tree, while the other is using a sharp one, the strength of the two men will make no difference as far as the result is concerned. The man with the sharp tool will do the better work, not because he has more muscle, but because he has a better ax. It finally dawned on me, with the force of a conversion experience, that I could never do much through the church because it is a dull instrument. That's the reason I joined the Salvation Army. It represented the sacrificial spirit of Christianity to me a hundred times more than the church.

"Take the church of St. Peter here in Champion, for example. It is always mentioned in the newspapers as the most fashionable church in town. Think of that! That's what the *News Crier* reported in its account of the annual meeting. What do the people know of sacrifice, or of the spirit of Christ, who gave up all His riches to become poor for the sake of dying humanity? I'm sitting in judgment on them, I know, and I will someday be called to account for doing so. But if I were a Catholic, I'd be willing to sit on the hottest fire in purgatory for the freedom to say what I believe about an 'aristocratic church.' And the one here in Champion is only one out of thousands across the country. What is the church, as an institution, doing to obey the command of Christ, to deny itself, take up its cross, forsake its ease and pleasure, and follow Him?"

Again Eric turned from his pacing and confronted Andrew. Stuart and Rhena watched him almost sorrowfully after listening to Eric's outburst. Over Andrew's usually jolly, good-natured face crept a gray shadow of seriousness that showed how deeply Eric's sharp condemnation had pierced him.

"Your question is larger than any answer I can make without taking hours to do so," he said at last, speaking calmly but with evident self-control over the fury of feelings he was experiencing. "The church today contains some of the noblest and some of the most petty of men and women. There is in the church the highest, purest, most saintly devotion to Christ and His teachings, and at the same time alongside it are the most awful selfishness and hypocrisy, and the love of ceremony and show. The scribes and Pharisees are just as much in evidence now as when they cried to Pilate, 'Crucify Him! Crucify Him!' Long ago I came to the conclusion that the same people would nail Jesus to the cross again if He appeared in this generation and denounced their hypocrisy and selfishness as He did before. At the same time, however, He would have a huge army of disciples who would suffer martyrdom for His sake. I see the church today as occupying a peculiar position in a struggling world between different groups of people.

"There is a growing feeling on the part of many churches that a great revolution in methods and purpose is at hand, and that nothing will be so radically changed in spirit and purpose as the church of Jesus Christ. The amount of relief for suffering that flows out of the organization we now have is no doubt enormous. Propose to any civilized community in this country that it wipe out its churches altogether, and the proposition would meet with instant objection even on the part of those who are most ready to denounce the church for its uselessness.

"I am not attempting to answer your question in full, Eric. Of course, if I did not believe in the church—I mean in its possibility to sacrifice—I would not use it as a center for my work. I would get out and work from some other basis. But this is my best reason for believing in the church as a power for the world's redemptive change after all else has been said and done."

Andrew paused, and the others listened thoughtfully. "The church is the only organization Jesus ever mentioned. He especially loved it, but it was not any particular form or name that He loved, but the idea of discipleship organized in love with one another and a common Master, going forward to conquer the world for God. And after the churches that have put Christ on trial or falsely represented Him have had their day, after the aristocratic churches have died and the memory of their pomp and ceremony is no more, after the coldness and carelessness and superficial worldliness of some churches have been played out, the true church will emerge. It will survive the wreck of all this agonizing death in life, and will be a true and universal representation of the crucified Lamb of God, giving its life for the needs of a suffering and dying world. 'I believe in the holy catholic Church'[1] in the sense that I believe it contains the leaven that is necessary to leaven the whole lump. Why, even the Salvation Army would never have come into being if not for the church."

"Do you mean that the church had grown so useless and petty that the Army had to be organized to do what the church ought to have done?" asked Eric with a smile.

"No, I mean that the Christian men and women who organized the Army had their nurture and training in the church. She was their mother. They went out from her home to do a work they never could have done if they had not been trained and taught at her feet."

"Isn't the Salvation Army as much the church as any other form of organization where Christian disciples get together in Christ's name?" asked Rhena.

"Yes, I believe that," replied Andrew.

"I mean to prove it by joining both," said Stuart, looking at Rhena.

"You can't join the Army without giving up your own wishes and being willing to obey the orders of your superior officer," said Rhena slyly.

"One of the other rules of the Army, I understand," added Andrew with a twinkle in his eye, "is a private cannot even marry without asking the permission of the commanding officer. Isn't that so, Miss Rhena?"

"I've asked permission and obtained it," said Stuart. "The commanding officer said, 'Get married as soon as you recover from your present illness.'"

"She did not!" said Rhena hastily. Then as Andrew and Eric began to laugh, she blushed and said, "Aren't we getting away from our original question? Stuart wants to know how to spend his money. It seems too bad if not one of us can tell him how."

"I can tell him how to use several thousand," said Eric who, after expressing his own mind on the church issue, was once more the calm, thoughtful, even congenial man he usually was. Eric had great strengths, but they were not fully developed.

"Well, go on!" cried Stuart.

"The miners need new houses in Cornish Town. What could be a better way to invest ten or twenty thousand dollars than to put up a hundred substantial houses that would really be homes?"

"What do you think of that?" asked Stuart, turning naturally to Rhena.

"It ought to be done," she answered softly, "and a good deal more. I'm not just thinking of the houses alone, but of the men, women, and children who live in them. There is no doubt they have lived for many years in the most miserable quarters. What can we expect of a family who lives in a cabin with three rooms at the most? How much refinement and civilization can come out of such sur-roundings? Stuart, you should drain the settlement area and—"

"I'll drain the whole neighborhood!" cried Stuart. "And the houses will be built immediately. Why have you let me lie here all this time, like something useless, when so much needs to be done?"

Just then Dr. Saxon arrived. He entered as usual, almost imme-diately after rapping on the door with his peculiar knock, known by everyone in Champion. He knocked and then entered, stopping only long enough to say, "It's the doctor."

The minute he walked into the room, Stuart began to abuse him for not getting him well more quickly. "I'm not going to pay you,

Doc, unless you give me something that will get me out of here in a day or two. Otherwise, I'll sue you for malpractice!"

"If you do, I'll sue your company for half a million dollars' worth of my work done on the miners since the strike and the fire. I'm going to retire after this winter if I can sue the company for what it owes me. Actually, you can get out again in a day or two. The only problem now is your heart trouble, and I can't cure that. You are in a very dangerous condition."

The doctor looked at Rhena and so did Stuart, and then after keeping a straight face for a moment or two, the doctor smiled and winked. To see him smile was rare, but it made his rugged, storm-beaten face appear quite handsome. He was already heading toward the door to leave, for he was in a big hurry that morning. He had stopped in simply to check on Stuart on his way up the hill.

"Stop him, please!" yelled Stuart to Eric. "Say, Doctor, don't go yet. We need your advice. We want your help in making plans for the relief—"

"Oh, please, get out of here with your plans for relief! I have no sympathy for these folks! The more you give these ungrateful, obstinate old . . . I tell you, Stuart, you'd better keep your money. You'll need it when you and Rhena take up housekeeping. Every time you go to town she'll want you to bring home a mousetrap, a lemon squeezer, or a jar of pepper or something. I'm leaving now. Eric, if you try to stop me, I'll throw you through the window."

The doctor rushed through the door and slammed it shut. A moment later he opened it again. Peeking in, he said in a serious tone, "If you plan to do anything worthwhile with the area that needs to be drained or build some new houses there, I'll give you a hint or two when I get time."

Instantly, he was gone again, and Stuart could see from the little window just a glimpse of Ajax and the carriage as they raced up the hill.

"I wonder if the doctor will ever take some time for himself," said Andrew. "And what will he do when he gets to God's perfect city, where there will be no more pain, tears, or death!"

"I'm at a total loss to even guess at what he'll do. I can't imagine him sitting on the edge of a rose-colored cloud taking it easy," replied Stuart. "But I have no doubt that God will make some special arrangements just for his benefit."

"Do you think we will all be as busy there as we are here?" asked Rhena.

"Of course," Andrew answered. "Only we will have plenty of time to do things exactly the way we want. I love to believe that I can grow roses of all sorts and have perhaps a thousand years to experiment on new varieties, without feeling all the time that I ought to be visiting a parishioner, writing a sermon, or getting ready for a committee meeting."

"You don't believe there will be roses in the next world, do you?" inquired Eric quizzically.

"I don't?" exclaimed Andrew. "What would heaven be without roses and little children?"

"I'm not arguing with your idea. I like it," replied Eric. "I hope there will be roses there, only without the thorns. But meanwhile, we are living in the town of Champion, where the thorns outnumber the roses two to one. If we make this little spot on earth more like heaven, perhaps we'll be better prepared to enjoy the next life more when our time comes to go."

"No doubt about it!" Stuart spoke with an emphasis that meant a world of action. "And as sure as the Lord is going to raise up this weak body of mine someday, I know I will give Him an account of my stewardship. So let's get to work! Eric, can you and Andrew begin arranging the details of this project? We need to build these houses as quickly as money can do it. While we're at it, let's tear down the other cabins and build new ones in their place. This is as clear as light to me. Our work is a necessity for these dear people."

"What about that hall dedicated to the interests of labor?" asked Eric, smiling.

"Up it goes, as soon as we can get to it. I don't like the idea of calling it a hall for labor, though. I tell you, Eric, the rich need preaching more than the poor do. They need to be taught the responsibilities that accompany their privileges. We'll build the hall, but it will be called the Hall of Humanity, and we'll dedicate it to the entire community. And whatever is said, preached, or sung inside it will be for the union of men—for their good as members of the human family. Every unselfish, Christlike word and deed we can think of will be given a place within its walls. Can you tell I've done some thinking about this since I've begun to get well? But first to building the houses! Rhena, we also need your help in the planning of this important housing project."

Rhena immediately began working on the plans for the houses with great enthusiasm. She outlined the most satisfactory and sensible arrangements for the structure of the new houses. And during the next few weeks she was the life of the project. Her wonderful common sense and practical knowledge of the needs of the people were great assets to Eric and Andrew as they coordinated the various other aspects of the project.

Two days after this discussion in Eric's cottage Stuart was able to go home. That evening he had an important conversation with Aunt Royal and Louise. Both of them had visited him several times while he was recovering at Eric's. And it was clear to Stuart that no plans he would undertake due to his new direction in life could possibly meet with their approval. The conversation began when Stuart mentioned his coming wedding plans.

"We'll get married as soon as Rhena's work will allow." Stuart was referring to her Salvation Army duties and her work with the building project.

"I suppose she is ordering her wedding gown from Paris? I would love to see a Salvation Army gown made after the latest European style," Louise said with a sneer.

"Do you plan to be married in the Army Hall?" asked Aunt Royal with a frigid look at her nephew.

"My wife," Stuart said with gracefulness that ignored their rudeness, but made one point very clear, "will be the undisputed mistress of this house. She is the equal of any woman alive in education, accomplishment, and grace. And she is the superior to most of them in her spiritual refinement and self-sacrifice."

"So you're planning to bring her here?" asked Louise with a curious look.

"Where else would I bring the woman I marry?" Stuart asked, turning to Louise.

"I just assumed Miss Dwight would prefer to live in a humbler fashion after all her talks and prayers about giving up this and that and the other. But, of course, if she decides to enjoy the sinful luxuries of life after roughing it in the Army halls, you know what I'll do?"

Stuart did not answer. Aunt Royal watched him closely.

"I will simply leave. That's all," continued Louise. "I won't live under the same roof with Rhena Dwight being a dictator over me."

Stuart was about to say something, but Louise interrupted him. "I'm able to take care of myself. Please don't argue with me, for I've made up my mind. Aunt Royal will let me stay with her until I am married. I'll be happy to go to New York. Besides, I'm getting tired of the winter up here, with everyone focused on all this gloom, sacrifice, and suffering. So don't postpone your happy wedding day on my account, Stuart."

"Louise, I want to speak to you privately a few minutes. Aunt

Royal," continued Stuart politely, but firmly, "will you kindly excuse me if I take Louise into the library?"

"By all means," replied Aunt Royal, who was outwardly cool and calm, but inwardly a raging fire.

Louise went with Stuart, although she resisted at first. Ultimately, there would have been no resisting his obvious determination to speak with her alone.

"Louise," Stuart began while facing the pretty countenance, as a look of pity and genuine love crept over his own, "I can't bear to think that we're going to let this misunderstanding separate us. Can't you and Rhena become friends?"

"No, it's out of the question," replied Louise curtly. She was thinking of the lie she had told Rhena. And she knew that whether or not Rhena was ready to forgive her, there was a great gulf between them, especially now that she was going to be Stuart's wife. Besides all this, Louise did not agree with any of his plans for his new life or money.

"Well, if that's out of the question, Louise, there's another matter I must address again. I'm referring to your promise to marry Hal Vasplaine. Be patient with me when I tell you, Louise, that out of the love I have for you, I would almost rather see you dead than married to that—"

"Is this why you called me in here?" cried Louise furiously, raising her voice. "I will not listen to it. You are a coward to attack him like this behind his back."

"Louise," interrupted Stuart, who was now deathly pale. "I'm saying this simply out of love for you. I forgive you for misunderstanding my motives," he added as he heard Aunt Royal nearing the door. "If the time ever comes when you feel the need of my love, my heart and home will always be open to you."

Louise turned from him and their conversation ended. It was just one more piece of evidence, daily growing stronger in Stuart's mind, of the vast difference between his old life and his new one. He now realized the true meaning of the verse, "A man's foes will be those of his own household." The battle line had been drawn the minute he chose to follow Jesus Christ, and the necessary separation between him and the old life continued to widen, as the situation with Louise and his aunt evidenced. He was not at all blind to the cause, for it was quite plain. He could not be a Christian and walk hand in hand with them, for the two paths led in exactly opposite directions. Yet this was only one test of his character, for he was to have a far more difficult choice to make at the end of the week.

The building of the new houses was proceeding as rapidly as circumstances would allow. A huge storm interrupted the work, and the deep snow was a serious hindrance. On top of this, there was the problem of finding construction workers during the frigid weather. The miners whose homes had been destroyed in the fire were being housed all around town. The hotel had provided some accommodations, but Stuart was actually footing the bill. The Salvation Army did its share, and then some. Yet the discomfort, crowding, and suffering were so great that money, even lavishly spent as Stuart was willing to do, could not provide much more than temporary and partial relief.

One afternoon at the end of the week, while Stuart was at the Salvation Army Hall working on better accommodations for the people, Eric rushed in. Rhena was working with some of the women at the other end of the hall as he arrived.

"The news from DeMott is serious," said Eric. "The men down there are threatening to pull up the pumps again. They are out of food and supplies and are starving."

"I can't feed the entire mining community, Eric!" said Stuart somewhat sharply.

"I know it." Eric sat down on a bench and put his face in his hands.

Immediately, Stuart felt convicted for his sharp words. "Forgive me, Eric. I spoke angrily. I will do everything in my power to help."

"It isn't that," replied Eric in a somber tone. "The men have refused to listen to me any longer and plan to act on their own! My authority with them has ended!"

"Nonsense!" But Stuart saw that Eric spoke the truth.

"It's true." Eric spoke with bitterness in his voice. "No one is as ungrateful as a mob of workingmen when it turns on its leaders. My time is over."

Just at that moment Andrew rushed in. "Have you heard the news?" he asked. "They say the DeMott men are going en masse to the Queen mine to pull up the pumps, and then to the Royal mine, and so on, until they have ruined every mine in these hills. They have given the companies two hours to concede to their terms."

Stuart thought for a moment and then said, "If they do something this serious, it will lead to an appalling loss of life. The Cleveland owners have kept the troops ready at Hancock because they have anticipated such a move. It's ridiculous for the men to think that the owners will yield to their demands at this late date."

"It will be a deathblow to labor and the workingman's cause forever if they do this," Eric said with a groan. "And here I am, helpless as a child. I . . ." Eric completely broke down and cried bitterly, feeling his time of leadership with the men had ended.

Andrew looked solemnly at Stuart. The short winter day was quickly coming to an end. Stuart stood there thinking, as he stared at the bowed form of Eric.

"There's one man who still has great influence over all the miners in Champion and DeMott," said Andrew gently.

Stuart quickly focused on Andrew, although he could see that Rhena had left her work at the other end of the hall and was coming toward him. Life seemed quite good to him now, so why should he risk it all? Going to the site of this latest controversy would mean placing himself in nearly certain danger. After all, was he his brother's keeper?

"That one man is you, Stuart," continued Andrew.

"You think I ought to go?" asked Stuart calmly.

"I cannot answer that for you," Andrew slowly replied.

"What are you talking about?" asked Rhena, joining the conversation as she walked up.

"Rhena," said Stuart, "it may be necessary for me to go to DeMott tonight. It looks as if the strike has reached a crisis point, and before morning something will probably occur to change the stable situation that has held all winter."

Rhena looked piercingly at the three men. "You're holding something back," she said at last.

"Yes," exclaimed Eric, lifting his head. "The men at DeMott are going to pull up the Queen mine pumps. I've lost my influence over them, and if Stuart goes there to stop the men, he will be risking his life. Many of the men will be drunk, and when they are, they are devils. They would kill anyone who goes there tonight to stop them, even if it were Christ Himself. Rhena, please stop Stuart from going. It means almost certain death. He will accomplish nothing but the loss of his own life."

Rhena did not say a word. Stuart looked at Andrew as if half hoping he would second Eric's plea. But Andrew was silent as well. Then Stuart turned toward Rhena again. He had never loved her as much as at that very moment.

"Rhena," he said in a soft voice, "I feel I ought to go to DeMott. I'm sure Eric is exaggerating the danger. And if I'm the only man with enough influence to prevent an uprising like this, am I not duty bound to exert that influence?"

"No! Don't go!" cried Rhena, and then she stopped. She had taken one step toward Stuart. She seemed to hesitate, as if searching for the right words, before finally saying, "I would never ask you to be a coward to please me. If you must go . . ."

"I must," replied Stuart. "God bless and keep you." He leaned over and kissed her, and without another word he stepped to the door and threw it open.

"I'll ask at the hotel's stable for a horse!" yelled Andrew to Stuart. But just at that moment Dr. Saxon drove up.

He's right on time, Stuart thought to himself, as if he had been expecting the doctor. He told Dr. Saxon the full story and how he needed to get to DeMott at once.

"Get in then! This means more gunshot wound practice for me perhaps." Rhena had stepped to the side of the carriage, pale and trembling. The doctor whispered to her, "Don't you worry, lass. The Lord protects drunkards and fools when they don't know enough to stay home nights. Whoa, now, Ajax!" he yelled at his horse, just long enough to allow Stuart to say good-bye to Rhena.

The next instant Stuart leaped into the carriage, and Ajax was suddenly flying over the road to DeMott. Andrew, Eric, and Rhena stood at the door of the hall watching until they disappeared. Finally, Rhena said, "Let's go inside and pray."

Andrew and Eric followed her inside. Andrew comforted her as they went, but Eric sat down moodily and was silent. While Rhena, some of the other women, and Andrew were praying together, Eric walked quietly from the hall. After looking around in the approaching dusk for a moment, he left. Walking briskly at first, he gradually increased his pace. He followed the tracks of the doctor's carriage, and he was soon running at full speed along the road to DeMott.

11

an
unexpected
orator

When Stuart and the doctor swept into DeMott after a fierce ride behind the now sweaty Ajax, they found nearly the entire population gathered around the large building adjoining the post office. Inside was a large hall that was used during the winter mostly for traveling business exhibits and shows.

It was packed tonight with the miners. The union was in session, and everyone who could find even a place to stand inside was there. The rest were waiting outside to hear the final decision. Each of them believed that the decision had already been determined, and that before morning every pump on the hillside would be pulled out and millions of dollars' worth of the companies' property would be destroyed in a few short hours. It would be the grim revenge of labor over management and would strike the owners at their most sensitive spot. For the miners it would seem to be a point of real satisfaction and payback for their terrible suffering during the winter. Far too many hollow-faced miners in the crowd could not help thinking of a little child lying dead under the snow in the large cemetery on the nearby slope. As a result, they grasped their clubs even more tightly and cursed the rich in their palaces of comfort that bitterly cold night.

Stuart had never felt more helpless. He looked at the faces around him, and his heart sank as he realized the tremendous power the mob had to do whatever it pleased. He felt that any influence he had in Champion would be perceived only as hollow words in DeMott. Surely, Andrew had been mistaken when he said Stuart could influence men like these, particularly at a time like this.

Stuart was jarred from his thoughts by the doctor, who spoke quickly and sharply. "Now then! Let's make a break for the hall! We'll leave Ajax right here."

Stuart was astounded and exclaimed, "They won't let us into the hall!"

"We'll see about that," replied the doctor.

He then drove Ajax to the front of one of the drugstores, where he typically hitched his carriage when he came to DeMott. He stepped from the carriage, with an awestruck Stuart following closely behind, and began to force his way through the crowd outside the hall. Yet as Stuart elbowed his way ahead, he began to realize that Andrew had been mistaken. If there was only one man left who had real influence over the miners, it was not Stuart Duncan, but Dr. Saxon.

It was almost comical to watch the change that came over the miners' faces as the doctor shoved men this way and that in order to get to the hall door. At first they swore and threatened to do unspeakable damage for the rough treatment they were receiving. But as soon as they caught sight of the doctor's rugged, kindly face, they were as polite and accommodating as if he had been a powerful king, and they his loyal subjects.

"Get out of the way, men! The doctor is needed in there! Someone must be hurt!" exclaimed a large Dane, who then grabbed another miner standing in front of the doctor and threw him aside by his collar, as if he had been nothing but a clothing store mannequin. In this way, the doctor, with Stuart struggling in his wake, fought his way to the hall door. Thirty years of absolute devotion to the many needs of the miners in DeMott and Champion had endeared the doctor to every one of the more than five thousand stubborn but strong, uneducated but warmhearted men in the mining community. Even tonight he was free to go wherever he wanted with no questions asked.

Finally, the doctor was in the hall with Stuart still behind him. For them to be there was contrary to union rules, but tonight there would be no strict enforcement of regulations. The miners were desperate and were resolved to do something, and they did not care who knew it.

The doctor remained silent, as he had been from the time he had started forcing his way through the crowd. He continued on through the men blocking the aisles. Stuart moved with the doctor, his mind in somewhat of a dream. He was amazed at the doctor's actions so far in pushing through the crowd, but had no real inkling as to his purpose in doing so.

Finally, they were on the platform, and the speaker stopped to shake hands with the doctor. Then Dr. Saxon asked in a quiet voice if he might say a few words to the men.

The chairman of the union happened to be one of the Champion men. It had been just two weeks earlier that the doctor had, as if by the sheer force of defiance over death, dragged the man's baby, at a critical time in its illness, from the very shadow of death into the warmth of life. He had traveled through one of the fiercest storms of the winter and waded through snowdrifts over his head, where even Ajax had refused to go. The chairman was a hard-faced, strong-fisted, but big-hearted Cornishman, who loved his children as much as any man on earth. And if Dr. Saxon had asked him for his last crust of bread, he would have said, "Take it all."

"Boys, Doc here wants to say a word or two. He don't belong here by the rules, but I say, let the doctor have his say!"

"Aye, aye! Let's hear the doctor!" shouted a hundred voices. The man who had been speaking sat down at once.

The doctor turned around and faced the men. It was a scene Stuart would never forget. It flashed through his mind like lightning that the doctor was taking this upon himself to save Stuart from the danger of a collision with the men. His love for Rhena nearly paled at this moment with what he was feeling for his dear old friend.

It was a scene for a master painter, although no painter could have caught the full meaning of it all. The doctor looked directly into the faces of the men. These were the same men by whom Dr. Saxon had stood as sickness or death had come to their little cabins, or when a horrible accident had come to the bottom of the mines. And they knew he was always the same in his unflinching devotion to performing his duty, in his unspoken love for the suffering, and in his wonderful skill to beat back death and look hell in the face without as much as blinking one eyelid.

"Now then," began the doctor in his usual abrupt manner, "there isn't a man here ever heard me try to make a speech in public, is there?"

It was very quiet in the hall. It was so quiet, in fact, that the noise of the crowd outdoors could be plainly heard. No one answered the doctor's question—they were all waiting to hear his next words. Usually, the men were not easily surprised, but the sight of the doctor in this setting was almost like seeing or hearing someone who had been dead for thirty years suddenly come back to life.

The doctor continued, "And I'm not going to make a speech tonight either. But I'm here to tell you, if you do what you're threatenin' to do, you'll be bigger fools than I've been calling you for thirty years or more. Why, you must be insane idiots—every last one of you—to think you can gain anything by pulling up those pumps! Who'll suffer? The mine owners? What if they do lose a little property up there? Haven't you got enough sense to know that it's only a drop in the bucket for them? But it's the whole bucket for you. And if you weren't such a lot of blockheaded dummies, you'd know that the result of pulling up the pumps will be to simply give me more work to do in mending your cracked skulls and sewing up a lot of gunshot wounds in your useless bodies.

"You need to know I've got my hands full already without having a lot of extra work piled on me. You'd better think before you decide to have a little picnic with those pumps, 'cause after you've pulled 'em up, and about a hundred of you are killed, or get what few brains you have left knocked out, what will you have gained? What chance at all will there be for mining in the spring with all the shafts flooded? Are you trying to kill me by causing more bloodshed?

"Tell you what I'll do. Any man here that wants me to amputate an arm or a leg, or fix his brains back into his empty head after he's gone and got himself mixed up in a fight with the militia, can just take my word for it here and now. I'll turn him over to these brand-new doctors that have been practicing on you since the fever struck this winter. Hear that? I simply won't do a thing for you!

"I'm as mad as you are at the mine owners. With the exception of Mr. Duncan here, I think the owners will have quite an account to settle on Judgment Day. But sure as death, you won't gain anything by trying to improve God's punishment for 'em. You know what'll happen if the mines stay closed into the spring. The owners will have to open 'em, but only if you leave the pumps alone. And you'll likely go back with an increase above your old wages. The pressure for ore will finally force the companies to reopen. But once you've ruined the mines, what will you do? Your babies are crying for food in the cabins now, you say. Well, it'll be worse then if . . ."

The doctor softened his voice for a minute, and the effect was magical. Stuart could not believe, and would not believe as long as he lived, that it was actually Dr. Saxon saying the next few sentences. And he never heard him with the same voice again. "The babies lying out there on that hillside will never hunger again. I have watched hundreds of them leave this unsatisfactory world this winter, and every single one of them pulled my heartstrings with his little fingers as death won him from me. But God is merciful. There is no doubt of His justice. There isn't a man here who doesn't know I love him and would never advise him to do something that was not for his own good and the good of his wife and children in the long run. Why, every one of you knows . . ."

At this point the doctor resumed his normal voice that the miners knew so well: ". . . even Ajax has more sense than to go and kick over the bucket that contains his oats. But that's what you plan to do. I always said that the stupidest numskulls that ever lived could be found in DeMott. I've looked into more cracked craniums here than anywhere else, and I've made up my mind that after this, when I've got broken heads to fix up, I'll use cotton or wool, or something like that, to stuff the vacant places I find."

Just then there was a disturbance by the door, and a voice broke the silence of the crowd, shouting, "Is the doctor here? He's wanted at once outside. There's been a fight, and Pat Penryck has got a broken head. Tell Doc to come right out!"

"Hear that!" roared the doctor. "If you pull up the pumps, I'll probably get shot by the militia myself just for tryin' to help you. And after I'm gone, who'll come and pump life into you when death has you by the throat? And if I don't get shot, I'm gonna leave you and go to Chicago, where I won't have to furnish the brains for the whole community!"

Without another word the doctor jumped off the platform and worked his way outside, where he cared for the wounded man as skillfully and tenderly as if his patient had been the president of the United States. At first Stuart had started to go with the doctor, but then suddenly changed his mind and stayed. The doctor had made a decided impression on the men. They were used to his rough, uncomplimentary denunciations, yet they loved him perhaps more than they loved anyone else. His blunt thoughts on the matter, even though flung so roughly at them, compelled them to think.

The next half hour in that old hall that night witnessed the closing chapter in the big strike. Man after man stood to declare that it would be madness to pull up the pumps. The doctor's words had struck into the heart of the matter, and men who had earlier sworn to destroy every cent's worth of mine owner's property they could lay hands on now urged caution and restraint. There was, however, one element they had not considered.

For several weeks the union had been close to dissolving. Eric had heard that news even before he was confronted with the loss of his own influence with the men, and he knew that the end was very near. The practical effect of this evening's event was to destroy whatever remained of the union. Stuart could also see the end coming. He leaned against the wall, forgotten by the union leaders and their men, as the debate continued.

There were several fiery appeals for carrying out the original plans of destroying the mines. The crowd seemed swayed back and forth as one after another of them spoke. Finally, the end came in a flash. A large, rugged man stood before the crowd. It was Sanders, whom the doctor had previously accused of using his prescribed cod-liver oil to shine his boots. In a booming voice that could be easily heard, although interrupted by his deep cough, he made a motion that the strike be ended.

As soon as debate began on the motion, pandemonium broke

out. News of the motion spread to the crowd outside, and it maddened the mob. They crushed toward the hall entrance until the chairman finally called for a vote after shouts of "Question! Question!" came from every direction. The motion was carried by a two-thirds vote.

Instantly, the men in the hall started to rush into the street, but were met at the entrance by the yelling crowd trying to get in. For several minutes there was a tremendous struggle, but gradually, the crowd outside, as it learned of the action of the union leaders, gave way. Once they heard that one of the most prominent miners in DeMott had called for the question as well, they began to calm.

In Stuart's mind there was no explanation for the union's vote, except that the men had increasingly grown more tired of the strike. They simply had been waiting for someone to make a break with the union rhetoric. Then they followed like sheep, and in less than ten minutes the union was history.

A few of the drunken men who were angered at the outcome of the vote that night went to the Queen mine determined to pull up the pumps and destroy as much as possible. The troops had anticipated such an attempt and drove the miners back, after a brief skirmish. Stuart did not learn of the episode until the next day, but fortunately, no one was killed. However, several had sustained head injuries by being beaten with clubs or by being pelted with chunks of ore. The doctor helped with the head injuries, grumbling as usual, and declared with each new case that it would positively be the very last he would handle.

Stuart left the meeting that night feeling that his part of the evening's work had been very insignificant. He had, in fact, been almost ignored in the excitement, and had been a silent spectator of the entire event. He had enough presence of mind to realize that the doctor's blunt statements, coupled with the miners' great love for him, were a tremendous influence on the final outcome. When

Stuart walked out to the street, the crowd was still discussing the situation in small groups, and everyone was wondering what the owners would do now.

Stuart was standing by the doctor's carriage, waiting for him to return, when a man touched him on the arm. He turned, and there stood Eric. He had run nearly all the way from Champion, although Stuart was unaware of that.

"Eric!" cried Stuart.

"I got here just in time to be of no use," said Eric flatly. Then he asked with more feeling, "You're not hurt, are you?"

"No. There's been no riot. Have you heard that the strike is over? How did you get here?"

"Yes, I heard the news quickly enough. I ran here. I'll never trust a crowd again. I thought I knew these men. I would have sworn nothing could prevent their pulling up the pumps tonight. I guess that shows how well I knew them."

"We can thank the doctor for the way things have turned out. You've never heard a speech like the one he gave tonight."

"No, and you'll never have the chance again," said the doctor as he walked up and began to untie Ajax. "It was my first and last time on any stage. And I wouldn't have gone up there this time, except I wanted to tell this good-for-nothing bunch what fools they are. I seldom have such a great opportunity to tell so many of 'em at once. Come on. Going back to Champion with me, Stuart?"

"Just a minute, Doctor! I'll be right with you!" yelled Stuart. He then pulled Eric aside and said, "Eric, you came here on purpose to share the danger with me. That means a lot." Eric did not answer. "I know you're feeling that the men were unjust with you by spurning your leadership. But don't let that make you bitter." Still Eric was silent. "Won't you ride back with us? We can make room."

"No, I'll stay here with some friends. I'll be back tomorrow," Eric replied as if with great effort.

Stuart laid a hand on his shoulder. "Eric," he said simply, "I love you."

Eric began to sob softly, and in the darkness a tear rolled down one cheek. He turned away and walked down the street, while Stuart left for Champion with the doctor.

"Eric's taking the loss of his influence with the men quite hard," said Stuart with a sigh.

The doctor replied somewhat curtly, "Thou shalt not put thy trust in the mob."

When they drove back into the square in Champion, the lights of the Salvation Army Hall were shining out a welcome. It seemed to Stuart as if the old weather-beaten building shone with the glory of the Lord. And no matter which way the union vote had gone that night, he felt secure in the love of at least one person—Rhena. She believed in him and his desire to be true to others, and she would willingly share any burdens, responsibilities, or privileges that came their way with this dramatic turn of events. A mutual faith in each other had sprung up in this man and woman, which helped make the great work that lay ahead of them possible. Rhena gained a new and even greater sacred respect that night for Stuart, who had been willing to risk his life for his call of duty.

The next few days in Champion and DeMott were full of excitement. The men flocked back to the mines and gathered around the little offices of the mine captains on the hillsides by the engine houses. But the Cleveland owners had not yet made any movement toward reopening the mines, and their captains in DeMott were awaiting orders.

Stuart was independent as far as his own mines were concerned, and remaining true to the promise he had made long ago, he posted notices that he would pay any miner in the Champion mines two dollars a day. Within a week he had more applicants than he could employ, so he quickly took steps to open new shafts that his father had begun. This provided jobs for another five hundred men, but when those in DeMott came over in droves, he was unable to employ even one-fifth of them.

He knew that he had made enemies of the other owners, and he anticipated a move on their part to ruin him commercially. But the longer they held out and refused to reopen or grant wages of two dollars a day, Stuart was in a position to gain many markets once closed to him. The demand for ore was growing daily, and it just so happened that the Champion mines produced a quite superior grade of ore. Therefore, Stuart could well afford to pay the wage of two dollars, whether the other mines opened or not.

As it turned out, the DeMott mines did not reopen for another two weeks. The Cleveland owners, after doing everything in their power to coerce Stuart to close his mines, finally realized that every day that passed only put him in a better position due to the rising market conditions. So they opened up a few mines with only a 10 percent increase in wages. This move, however, nearly led to another strike and formation of another union. But the long winter; sitting idle for so long, which was so unusual for the men; and the great financial losses they had sustained took their toll. The DeMott men returned to work a few at a time.

This brought about something never before seen in that iron region: nearly fifteen hundred men receiving two dollars a day in Champion, and twice that many men receiving one dollar and ninety cents on the lower range of hills. At the end of two months, once lake navigation had resumed, ore rose so high in price that the DeMott mines raised their wages to two dollars as well. The men received, largely through Stuart's efforts in standing firm, the amount they had originally demanded. But there was no great celebration over the victory because the strike had been too costly. Suffering had left its mark on every home, and the men were in no condition, when the increase in wages came, to expend much energy gloating over it.

Long before all this had happened, Stuart and Rhena had begun planning for their new life together. One day soon after the Champion mines had opened they were in Cornish Town looking at the new cottages being built. They had pushed hard to get the houses constructed quickly, and they were seeing great results. In fact, most of the houses would be ready for use within two weeks. After giving some specific instructions to one of the workmen, Stuart asked Rhena to walk up the trail with him to the old stump where he had first told her he loved her.

When they reached the stump, they turned to look down at the town. It was still winter, and the snow was deep throughout the valley. The sound of the workmen rose to them from Cornish Town. Smoke from the engine house smokestacks wafted across the range of hills. And all the stockpiles of ore were dotted with men happy to be working once more.

Stuart, pointing to the stump, said, "I believe I'll put a little cottage right here, and we can begin housekeeping on a modest scale like the rest of the people down there. What do you think of that?"

"But wouldn't we be putting ourselves *above* them if we build up here?" asked Rhena slyly.

"No, we would simply be in a position to see all of them, and we would be better able to help them in times of need."

"I don't think this stump is quite large enough for a foundation," said Rhena jokingly, but with a straight face. "Why, after I opened the front door, I'd have to go outside again to shut it."

"You are very hard to please, madam," replied Stuart. "What do you want? A palace? I thought a Salvation Army girl would be ready to put up with almost anything!"

"Stuart," Rhena said in a serious tone, "I could be happy with you in any one of the cottages down there, and you and I know that. But the Army is very dear to me. I can't leave it."

"I'm not asking you to leave it," replied Stuart, smiling. "I first fell in love with your bonnet, and I hope you will wear it at our wedding."

"I'm just thinking of the poor men and women I have been living with for so long," continued Rhena. Her eyes filled with tears. "I can't bear to have them think that because I'm going to be the wife of a mine owner and live in his house, I'm going to be so far above them that . . . Stuart, do you know what I mean? If I didn't believe so completely in you and your beliefs regarding the stewardship of God's property, I would not dare to marry you—a man with so much money and such a fine house. I can hardly even think of such elegant living without shuddering."

"We need great wisdom to use God's blessings. It will be a joy for us to work out the problem together, won't it?" He had spoken so softly that with the exception of Rhena, only a snowbird on a nearby fir tree could have heard it. And the bird will never tell.

Their wedding was scheduled for the following week. They stood on the upper trail for some time discussing the approaching event, before Stuart changed the topic to say, "Louise and Aunt Royal are going to New York the first of the week. My only regret, Rhena, is my being unable to reconcile them with us. We just live in a different world from theirs."

"I'm sure you've done everything you could, Stuart," replied Rhena gently. Yet she was preoccupied with another matter. She asked, almost timidly, "The Army asked me if I planned to be married in the church. Would you mind, Stuart, if we were married in the old Army Hall?"

"No," said Stuart. Besides, he was, and had always been, indifferent to the various ceremonies of life, even the high societal life from which he was now free. And he understood the reason behind her request. She belonged to the Army, and the small squad of officers and privates was very dear to her. She longed to assure them in every possible way that her marriage would not separate them from her in the least.

One evening about a week later, and after the departure of Louise and Aunt Royal, Stuart went to Eric's cottage. There he met Andrew and the doctor, and together they went to Rhena's boarding-house. Soon she came out dressed in her Army uniform, which Stuart said was the best and most appropriate outfit for her to wear. She took his arm, and with Eric, the doctor, and Andrew walking closely behind, they proceeded to the Army Hall.

The Army members were very excited. They had marched the streets, held their outdoor meeting, and were already back to welcome the bride- and groom-to-be. The small group stood just outside the door, and what it lacked in numbers, it made up for in strength. The bass drum had never received such a vigorous beating as it got that night, and the poor tambourines would have been knocked to pieces if they had not been made of very tough materials. And "Crusty Joe," now known as "Witnessing Joseph," played his flute so hard that if he had not been blessed with such a huge pair of lungs, he would have nearly blown himself through the holes of his instrument.

Surrounding the Army band, also on the street outside the hall, was a huge crowd of the miners of Champion. They greeted the small bridal party with hearty cheers as it arrived; and as soon as the band had finished, and Stuart, Rhena, Andrew, Eric, and the doctor had gone in, they crowded into the hall. It would have been impossible for the building to hold even one more person.

There were many brief prayers and several lively songs once the Army took its place on the platform. The major, who seemed somewhat carried away by the greatness of the occasion, made a stirring speech, which was punctuated with frequent "Amen's" and "Hallelujah's" from the rest of the Army. And although the service was a wedding, a collection was taken on behalf of the Army's ministry. Since this was a special occasion, and due to the fact that the men were once again at work, the tambourines were heavy with silver. The major could not help thinking of immediately using the money to build a suitable headquarters.

The crowd quieted and the actual wedding service started. Andrew began speaking to Rhena and Stuart, who stood in the middle of the platform, while Eric and the doctor stood to one side behind Stuart. The ceremony did not follow the usual Salvation Army rules, but as "Witnessing Joseph" said in a few remarks after the offering was taken, "Anything goes tonight!" Andrew's prayer for the couple was beautiful and full of power, and the major later remarked, "That prayer was nearly as good as any we've had here, even on confession night."

Stuart was impressed by the entire ceremony, in spite of the old, run-down surroundings and some of the Army rituals. The woman standing next to him in the Army uniform, who had pledged to walk hand in hand with him through life, made up for any possible shortcomings. The sinners and the suffering of humanity, many of whom were crowded around them in the hall, had become their primary focus. It seemed especially appropriate to Stuart that they would share the most sacred event of their lives in the presence of those they desired to help. They truly regarded the miners as belonging to the great brotherhood of the family that is one in God the Father.

They had planned on remaining for some time to shake hands with the men inside after the service was over. But the crowd outside was clamoring to get in, and finally, at the major's suggestion, the men filed up to the platform, shook hands, offered their greetings, and went down the other aisle and back outside. The men still standing in the street then formed a line that reached into the town square and past the stage. And before Stuart and Rhena realized what had happened, they were facing a steady stream of well-wishing miners that would take two to three hours to greet.

"Can you handle this, Mrs. Duncan?" asked Stuart, looking into her blushing face, which had never looked as beautiful in its Army bonnet as it did tonight.

"You forget, sir, that I have stood in this hall many long hours this winter. I'm quite confident that you will be tired before I am. Isn't this beautiful of them? This is worth more, Stuart, than all the pomp and circumstance of high society—for these people love us and we know it."

"Yes, indeed!" exclaimed Stuart proudly, happy for his wife's strength, beauty, and Christian character. "These men truly belong here tonight. This is worth a million times more to me than all the elaborate trimmings of society's fashionable weddings."

Meanwhile the doctor, Andrew, and Eric had seemed to disappear. But when Stuart and Rhena came out after receiving the men, and after some final joyful shouts and drumbeats from the Army, they found the three men by the side of a beautiful new carriage trimmed with spruce boughs. The doctor motioned for them to take a seat as he sat on the driver's bench.

"What!" cried Stuart. "You're still here, Doctor? When I didn't see you, I thought surely you had been called away."

"It's a wonder I wasn't," replied the doctor. "All through the ceremony I thought I could hear a voice saying, 'Is the doctor in there? He's wanted at once. Lew Trethven's broken his leg and wants the doctor to come right up.' Now then, are you ready? Eric and Andrew are going with me to escort you home. We were afraid you might lose your way."

"Do you dare ride with the doctor?" Stuart asked Rhena.

"I dare to go anywhere with you," she replied. For that answer, the crowd excused Stuart for kissing her in public as he lifted her into the carriage.

The doctor had hitched Ajax to the fastest horse he could find in the hotel stables, and after they had started, he realized he had his hands full. The miners let out a cheer as the new couple dashed through the square and out onto the road leading up to the Duncan house. And so, wrapped in the love of the men whose lives and happiness were forever to be deeply linked with theirs, and in the company of friends who had greatly shared in their life-changing experiences, this man and woman began their new life together. Their friends would mean even more to them in the coming days, but this couple were beginning a life as man and wife that even death could not separate, for they were one in Jesus Christ.

Exactly one week to the day later, in a large mansion on a fashionable avenue in New York, Louise Duncan and Hal Vasplaine were married. Aunt Royal, at whose house the event took place, sent Stuart a card announcing the wedding. The notice was addressed simply to Stuart, did not include Rhena, and arrived two days after the fact. It was the first he had heard of their marriage, and in fact, he was unaware that they had set a date. He was deeply grieved over his sister's marriage to Vasplaine, and he felt that the rift between his sister and himself had reached an impasse. But the rest of his life was filled with joy. Rhena meant everything to him, and as time went on he felt the intense pain over his relationship with Louise begin to lessen. Yet he never ceased to pray for his sister or to love her for even one moment.

The demands on Stuart and Rhena certainly did not seem to lessen, although the mines were open again. The new cottages were complete, but Stuart was contemplating rebuilding all of the cottages on the nearby range of hills. This idea, however, met with unexpected and irritating resistance from the miners, who did not want their lives to be disrupted.

"They're the most ungrateful bunch on earth," said the doctor, with whom Stuart had shared his idea. "If I were you, I'd hire someone to torch every last cabin some windy night and burn up every last one of 'em—that is, the cabins. They—I mean the men—haven't got brains enough between them all to win a debate with a feebleminded old woman!"

Stuart was wrestling with how to handle this problem, yet at the same time was moving ahead with his plans for the Hall of Humanity. Many long meetings were held in Eric's cottage, Andrew's room, or Stuart and Rhena's house to discuss the project.

During one of those meetings, Rhena proposed another project, which was at first strongly opposed by Eric and Andrew, but finally received their heartfelt support. The idea was to turn the Duncan mansion into a modern hospital operated by Dr. Saxon. The house seemed too large to be a residence for only two people. Besides, Stuart and Rhena wanted to be closer to town, and Stuart had already begun planning a house that would more closely represent what they believed a home should be. This would enable them to be used in more ways because their current house seemed too far away from the people.

Rhena remained very involved in the work of the Army, and the people knew by now that her marriage had not lessened her love for them or her desire to see them saved. In fact, Stuart and Rhena desired to do everything in their power to use their wealth to the greatest advantage possible. Their old mansion was well suited to be a hospital, and their plans for it came together quite well. And Dr. Saxon certainly seemed entitled to a role that would allow him to spend the remainder of his life usefully and peacefully.

One evening in the early spring, Stuart and Rhena were discussing their various plans. The foundation for the Hall of Humanity was being built, and they were reviewing all the things they hoped the building would represent. The lights were on in their house, as it was fairly late in the evening, and a soft rain was falling outside, although the wind through the pines indicated the approach of a heavier storm. Stuart was seated at the dining room table with their plans scattered across it. Rhena was excitedly walking back and forth, quite enthused over their ideas, when the doorbell rang.

Stuart, sensing something was wrong due to the late hour, went to the door. As he threw it open, the wind blew a fine mist of rain into the foyer, along with the fragrant aroma of the dripping pines. Yet he was suddenly conscious of only one thing.

Before him on the stone steps lay the shadow of a woman. As he stooped to lift her, he realized that his sister had remembered that she would always be welcome in his home—just as he had promised. Here she was—so soon! He carried her into the very room where their father had died and laid her on the same bed. As he did so, and as Rhena gently pulled her wet overcoat from across her face, Louise moved. She then opened her eyes to look at Stuart and Rhena, and they will never forget that look. It told them, even more plainly than words could ever tell, Louise had come home to die.

Yes! The enemy of this world is very bitter when it comes. And it always comes, in God's time.

12

true
stewardship

For a moment Louise looked at Stuart and Rhena as if she knew them. Then she sat up, partly supporting herself with one hand, and with the other seemed to reach for something. Yet there was a look of madness in her eyes.

"Father! He's hurt! Don't you know, Stuart? The horses ran away. We were thrown out! Why doesn't someone send for the doctor?"

Rhena slipped from the room and telephoned Dr. Saxon. Stuart fell on his knees by the bed, and the next half hour was one of the most agonizing he had ever known. Louise ranted and raved and wept. She seemed to be reviewing days gone by, and repeated many conversations word for word between Stuart and herself around the time he had begun his new life, which was also near the time of Ross Duncan's death. Mingled in, however, were a number of experiences in her life since leaving Champion. Some of them literally made him shudder, and he put his hands over his ears to keep from hearing more painful news. Stuart did not dare to imagine the full meaning of Louise's words.

When Dr. Saxon finally reached the house and entered the

room, Louise was simply lying there moaning. The doctor stepped to the side of the bed and spoke her name. She opened her eyes, looked him full in the face, and then screamed out hysterically, "Doctor! Doctor! Save me! I'm going mad! I am mad!"

"You poor child!" was all he said.

Then Louise began to cry uncontrollably. She spoke Aunt Royal's name so chillingly that it even made the doctor shiver somewhat. Then as quickly as if she had been made suddenly mute, she fell back as if dead and lay so still that at first Stuart thought the end had come already.

Stuart and Rhena stood there stunned and pale. The doctor did everything in his power, but there was really not much he could do. After thirty minutes Louise awoke from her apparent state of exhaustion and cried out once again, this time screaming Vasplaine's name with such terror that Stuart could not endure it. He went into the room across the hall and was followed by Rhena.

"This is awful!" Stuart said with a groan. "What do you suppose all this means? What has that criminal done?"

"It means that he has left her, and that—" Rhena stopped abruptly. This was simply speculation on her part, since Louise was unable to share the details of her situation. Certainly, all this had been a sudden blow to Stuart and Rhena.

"Please, God! Save her life!" he cried.

"And restore her mind," added Rhena gravely.

They then returned to Louise and sat with her and the doctor throughout the night. The doctor was concerned that if she were left alone, she might try to leave the house in the midst of the powerful storm that seemed to be relentlessly pounding the mansion. The large pine trees outside swayed and sobbed like a requiem over dead hopes and buried loves.

With the first gray light of morning the doctor noticed a change in Louise's condition. He had watched her all night, but now walked to the library and signaled for Stuart to follow him.

"She's out of immediate danger," he said. Stuart stood there by him, worried and weary from the strain of the night. "She's had some terrible mental shock, and it's doubtful she will recover. But she's a Duncan, so all things are possible! I think she'll remain quiet during the day, but if she's not, please send for me at once."

The doctor compassionately squeezed Stuart's hand and then drove to town through the raging storm. An hour later Stuart saw him racing up the hill and past the mansion on the Beury road to help with some emergency case in the hills. How the doctor lived without sleep was always a mystery to everyone in Champion.

Louise continued in a mental stupor throughout the day and the following night. Occasionally, when Stuart would call her name, she seemed to know him, yet she never expressed any surprise at being back in her old house. Gradually, the truth became evident to Stuart and Rhena that nearly everything since Louise's marriage was a complete blank to her. She would lie there silently for hours, without any expression whatsoever in her eyes. Her large eyes were still beautiful, although her once lovely face had grown old and haggard. When she did speak, it was in the irritating and complaining voice she had often used before, whenever Stuart had angered her.

To his great surprise and relief, however, she did not appear to dislike Rhena. She accepted Rhena's gentle, loving care as a matter of routine, and showed neither gratitude nor resentment. She was growing weaker, yet more and more demanding as time went by, so that Rhena's energy was stretched to the limit in attempting to meet her many wants. She asked constantly for the most expensive and difficult foods to be prepared, demanded costly flowers for her room, and was continually begging Stuart to buy her jewels to wear.

Finally, he went to town and removed a diamond necklace, a string of pearls, a ruby bracelet, and several turquoise rings from his office safe. He had kept the jewelry there ever since his mother's death. Ross Duncan had bought them for his wife once he was able to boast a net worth of a million dollars. The total value of these few pieces alone could have kept a dozen families living in comfort their entire lives. Yet Mrs. Duncan had not cared much for these "playthings," as she called them, and had seldom worn them. Ross Duncan had willed them to Stuart instead of Louise because of a simple thought he had one day. He said they were family jewels and ought to remain with the son of the house.

Louise was thrilled with these elaborate jewels and exhibited an eagerness to flaunt them. Stuart thought her obsession with the jewelry was quite shameful. She first wore the diamonds and then the pearls around her pale, thin neck, eventually wearing them both at the same time, as well as the bracelet and all the rings. She continually begged for new dresses, so at Stuart's suggestion, Rhena found some of his mother's silk gowns that had been packed away in a chest in the attic. By altering the dresses somewhat, they were made to fit Louise, and although she was only able to sit up for a few hours a day, she seemed to take a sad but childish delight in wearing the fine clothing. With Rhena's help in holding a hand mirror, she would constantly look at herself while pridefully commenting on her own appearance.

One day Rhena slipped away from Louise, and as she was going into the library, Stuart came in from the dining room, where he had been reviewing the new building plans again.

"Oh, Stuart!" Rhena sobbed as she closed the door so Louise could not hear her. "This is horrible! Dressing her like this is like clothing death itself in tinsel and glitter. The mockery of it makes my heart ache! I wish we knew the real cause of her problems. Then perhaps we could bring her back to sound thinking. Only—"

"Only what, dear?" Stuart asked, taking her in his arms to comfort her. He was thinking how caring Rhena had been to so faithfully care for his sister.

"Only—I fear the end is not far off. She is wasting away like snow on the hillside in spring."

Stuart groaned. "I know, dear. The doctor has done all he can, yet he offers no hope." He fell silent for a moment before saying with a calm strength, "I'm going to New York to see Aunt Royal and will get to the bottom of this problem. I've written her but received no reply, and all of my efforts to find Vasplaine have failed as well. Even his family can't find him. I will combine this trip with some necessary planning for the new building and will return within the week."

Stuart arrived in New York just before Aunt Royal had planned to pack her trunks and go abroad for the summer. One of the servants ushered him into the huge living room of her mansion, and he stood by the window awaiting Aunt Royal. His heart was heavy as he thought of Louise. He tried to compose himself for what he knew would be a difficult discussion, and he thought of his Christian faith and what it would demand in these circumstances.

When she finally appeared, he was surprised, for he had not heard her approaching the room. The velvet carpets of the home were bought to cover and to deaden the footsteps of a gardener's daughter who had made her money by investing in tenements and saloons.

"This is an unexpected pleasure, Stuart, to be sure," said Aunt Royal in her usual polite and gentle voice.

"You know why I'm here, Aunt Royal," Stuart said flatly, immediately coming to the point.

"No, I can't say that I do. I suppose you're here on some business related to your philanthropic plans in Champion. I hear the strike has ended. I suppose the miners have learned a lesson by their foolishness."

"Aunt Royal," Stuart said firmly, ignoring what she said, "I've come here to learn the truth about Louise. Tell me what you know about it. Perhaps it will help us to restore her mind before she dies. For God's sake, if you know something, tell me!"

Aunt Royal's face seemed to pale slightly. "Restore her mind?"

"Yes," replied Stuart sternly, "she's out of her mind. Her memory of anything since her marriage is a total blank. She must have received some great shock. Of course, we know now that Vasplaine has deserted her and cannot be found anywhere. And she is dying. After all . . . if . . ." Stuart paused, and his heart almost stood still as he caught the expression on Aunt Royal's face. He was not looking directly at her, but at her reflection in a large full-length mirror. It was the reflection of an absolutely selfish and heartless woman. She fully enjoyed her social standing, and she was totally unmoved by worldly sins or the misery and pain of a dying humanity.

Aunt Royal's voice came to his ears with its usual placid smoothness. "Louise left here for her honeymoon tour immediately after her marriage. They went south and then took a trip out West. When they returned, they booked a suite in a nearby hotel. I saw them often, but only on casual occasions. Vasplaine had begun to drink and trouble soon followed. When he finally left her, I was as surprised as anyone."

She paused suddenly, and Stuart remained silent as well. A large gold clock on the marble mantel dropped a silver ball into a bowl, and Aunt Royal turned her head slightly toward it. But Stuart was still focused on her reflection in the mirror.

"When did Louise leave New York for Champion?" he finally asked.

"I don't know anything about it," replied Aunt Royal with the first hint of irritation she had shown.

"Do you mean to say, Aunt Royal, that after Vasplaine deserted her, Louise never came to see you?" Stuart asked. He then turned to look straight in her face as resolutely as if he already knew the answer.

Once again Aunt Royal's face seemed to pale. Even after so many years of faking calmness at high society events, she could not control her inner feelings and her blood pressure.

"I'm telling you I did not see her after Vasplaine so disgracefully deserted her. He turned out to be a heavy gambler and an indulgent fool of the worst kind, throwing Louise's property and money around like a madman. I don't know where he is now."

"I didn't ask about him," said Stuart dryly. "I'm simply concerned about Louise."

He thought for a moment in silence, but could not help believing that his aunt was lying. Yet he was powerless to prove it. Finally, feeling sick over the thought of being so openly lied to, he wanted to escape from her house.

"Won't you stay for lunch?" Aunt Royal asked politely as he started to leave.

"No, thank you," replied Stuart softly. "I must head back to Champion this afternoon."

"I hope poor Louise will recover," Aunt Royal said. She was about to add something when one of her servants came into the room to tell her she had an important telephone call. It had something to do with her proposed summer tour abroad.

"Excuse me while I answer this. If you don't mind, I'll let you see yourself out," she said in her conventionally polite tone and was gone.

Stuart was just heading out when the servant who had opened

the door for him quietly said, "I can tell you something about your sister, sir, if you will wait a minute."

"Of course, I want to know all I can." Stuart was surprised and initially thought the man might simply be sharing some gossip he had overheard, or was trying to make some extra money. But hoping the information might be helpful to Louise, he stayed to listen.

"I don't have time to tell you the full story," the man quickly whispered, "but Mrs. Vasplaine came here one night about a week ago, and I couldn't help hearing what happened in the living room. She begged her aunt to take her in and shelter her till she could find another place. Her husband had run off with another man's wife and had gambled all her money away. As nearly as I could make out, the poor woman was almost crazy over the shame and ruin of it all.

"She begged and begged, but her aunt wouldn't even consider taking her back because it was so scandalous. Your aunt was concerned about how her society friends would view it, so finally Mrs. Vasplaine went away. She looked to me like she might drown herself. I felt so sure of it that I slipped out the back way and followed her. I saw her take a bus and have not seen her again. This is the honest truth. I don't mind telling you because I'm taking another job this week anyway. Begging your pardon, sir, for I know she's your relative, but I'd rather work for the devil himself than for your aunt."

Stuart tightly clenched his fists, and in his heart he uttered a groan. To his surprise, there stood Aunt Royal—her face flaming. She had entered the foyer through a side door directly behind the servant. Stuart was unsure how much of the man's story she had heard, but it was certainly enough to let her know that Stuart knew the truth as well.

"It's all a lie, a miserable lie!" she screamed.

This was the first time Stuart had ever seen such passion in his aunt. His back was to the front door, and for a moment he just looked at her. Then without saying a word, he turned around, opened the door, and walked out.

The warm sunshine seemed like something almost human as he closed that door behind him and walked away. At least he knew the truth, and there was no doubt in his mind that Louise had been denied shelter in her greatest time of need by this lady of society. This so-called lady would risk hell itself rather than the possible loss of her standing in society and her selfish life of ease and pleasure. And although Stuart had immediately believed the servant's story, it was later confirmed to him through his various New York acquaintances.

Before returning to Champion, he was gradually able to piece the full story together of how Vasplaine had ruined Louise financially and had then brutally abandoned her. She had found herself practically without friends in New York. So with Aunt Royal as her only nearby relative, it was quite natural for Louise to turn to her in her time of crisis. By the time she did, however, she was very possibly mentally crazed by the succession of tragic events that had come her way. Initially, Stuart was amazed at how quickly Vasplaine had gotten possession of Louise's money and squandered it. But the more he learned of Vasplaine's past, the less surprised he was. Louise had trusted the man, and she was fascinated by a certain attractiveness such men often seem to possess. Once he left her, she was ruined and found herself alone in a huge and faceless city.

Aunt Royal's refusal to provide her shelter became the final straw for her burden of shame and misery. Stuart would never learn what had transpired between the time that Louise had left her aunt's and had appeared so unexpectedly in Champion. But there were at least two days when she must have wandered aimlessly or perhaps had taken the wrong train to return home. She must have been quickly losing her ability to reason, yet was just able to hang on long enough to find her way back to Stuart's doorstep that stormy night.

All this caused Stuart some bitter thoughts as he hurried back to Champion. He almost dreaded getting off the train for fear the doctor would meet him as he had before when his father had died. But no one was there with any news, and when he reached the house, he was surprised to find Louise sitting up and looking no worse than when he had left. He tried to show courage and hope for her sake, for the doctor said she might linger through the summer, but would never recover mentally. In spite of this constant shadow of death in their home, Stuart and Rhena continued with their great plans for serving the people of Champion. Caring for and attending to Louise only strengthened and refined their love for each other and their fellowmen.

Work on the Hall of Humanity was continuing rapidly, and Stuart was determined to have it ready for its dedication before winter set in, if at all possible. He had employed a very large force of the best workmen he could find. Of course, getting to this point meant that he, Andrew, Eric, the doctor, and Rhena, along with many other good people in town, had put a great amount of time, effort, and thought into the plans and purposes of the building. The Hall of Humanity stood on one side of the square almost opposite St. John's Church, on a site where Stuart had torn down several smaller buildings he had previously owned. At the same time the hall was being built, Stuart was laying the foundation of his new home nearby.

A few days after Stuart's return from New York, Eric and Andrew had come to the Duncan mansion at Stuart's request. They were sitting with him and Rhena in the library and were discussing the plans that were finally beginning to take shape. Eric had returned to work in the mines with the other men, but still seemed to be experiencing some bitterness over his humiliating loss of influence with them. He had been able to attend this meeting with the others due to a miners' holiday being celebrated that day.

"I'm not sure I fully understand this part," said Andrew, who was examining the plans of the hall that were spread out before him on the table. Stuart explained Andrew's specific concern, and then they all began to talk about the building's purpose once again.

"How do you see this being used exactly?" asked Eric as he pointed to the part of the plans indicating a huge auditorium.

Stuart responded, "I don't know that I have very many 'exact' ideas about any of the future uses of the building, except that I want it to represent, in general, the word *helpfulness*. I've been thinking of the wonderful singers, stage actors, and lecturers who understand and agree with our purpose, and who could be obtained for modest fees. I believe we could attract some of the best talent in music, drama, and lecturing from around the world, and give the miners of Champion a taste of some of the world's best. And I believe we could pack this hall with men, women, and children by keeping the costs within their reach. Then I would see art exhibits here once or twice a year, and of course, flower shows about four times each year. You see, Eric, I'm a convert to your idea of music and flowers for everyone. We could even allow Andrew here to run the flower show if he would promise not to turn the place into an extravagant hothouse."

That last idea excited Andrew so much that he got up and began to pace the room. "My!" he exclaimed. "Just think of a hall this size filled with chrysanthemums, roses, and orchids! You'll allow me a few orchids, won't you, Stuart?"

"Just a minute here!" cried Rhena. "Stuart, don't let Andrew spend all our money on orchids first thing. He's pretty extravagant! Think of all the dollars it will take to handle these events. And quite honestly, I've questioned the practicability of all these rooms connected to the main hall."

"Why, you did the planning for them yourself, Rhena. What's the matter with them?" questioned Stuart.

"All I'm questioning is how much all these different things will really help the people. Here, for instance, is the space we have allocated for the Salvation Army Hall. I admit it looks beautiful on paper, and it will no doubt look fine when it is actually built in wood and stone, but will the Army feel at home in it? Will they be able to reach the same kinds of people who now come into the old hall?"

"I'm not understanding your criticism. What do you want us to do—build an Army Hall that looks old, like the shanty we already have? Should we knock out a dozen panes of glass and stuff the miners' old clothes into holes in the wall simply to make it feel like home?"

"There's a good deal of common sense in what your wife says, just the same," said Andrew. "If the Salvation Army becomes too refined, it won't be the Salvation Army anymore, and it won't do the Army's work."

"Christ wore good clothes, didn't He?" asked Eric bluntly.

Everyone was silent for a moment. They all knew what he meant, and yet the Army *did* have a distinct way of reaching humanity. Who could tell what the result might be if that special way were disturbed or changed?

"Don't worry about that," Stuart said thoughtfully. "If using a decent, well-lit, and heated room with plenty of chairs destroys the Army's usefulness, we'll return them to the old barracks they've used for years. Rhena and I have discussed this many times. It's the only thing we've ever disagreed about, and yet we've reached some common ground on it."

"These kindergarten rooms on this side of the building are going to be wonderful!" cried Andrew with enthusiasm. The idea for the rooms had been his, and he had supervised the planning of their specifications.

"I agree!" cried Eric. "I'm like the doctor in believing many of these older folks in town are fools or numskulls. But it's the children who are the hope of the whole labor issue if they are given the right opportunities from the start."

By this time they were all leaning over the table and eagerly discussing the numerous features of the hall and its various uses. There were to be beautiful reading rooms and a library, rooms for social gatherings, a gymnasium, an art gallery, a photography studio, and even rest rooms. They were also planning various classrooms, which could be used for training whenever they needed to reach beyond their current abilities, talents, and skills.

"There is something we haven't thought about," Eric said with some sadness in his voice. "What practical use can these people make of all these things we're providing if they are still going to spend the better part of their lives underground, at least during the daylight hours? And won't exposing their minds to all these finer things in life simply breed a discontent that will result in more misery than they have today?"

"You old pessimist!" Stuart exclaimed. "Would you tell the human race, 'Don't smell that pretty flower today because you may not have any tomorrow, and that will make you discontented'? Just because a man's life is devoid of anything pleasant, should we keep him in that condition, lest he grow discontented by knowing something better?"

"That's right!" exclaimed Rhena, her eyes flashing. "Eric knows better than to talk that way. Think what these men have missed all their lives! I would think you would want them to experience these things. And regarding how much time they spend underground— Stuart, you need to work with labor to find a way to provide more leisure time, so they can see more of God's green earth when the sun is still shining upon it."

"Hear! Hear!" agreed Andrew. "'Bring me,' as Aladdin said to the genie in his lamp, 'thirty golden dishes full of pearls, and as many more full of diamonds.'"

"What Rhena asks for labor is obviously impossible right now," responded Stuart. "But there's no reason for it to always be this way. After all, why should many thousands of human beings dig below ground in the dark, in constant and deadly danger, and separated from most of the pleasures of earth, simply so men like me may lead a more comfortable life?"

"Because they don't know how to do anything else and wouldn't if they could," said Eric bluntly.

"You don't know that, Eric," Stuart retorted. "You just think that because they've never done anything else."

"Well, someone has to do the mining," Eric responded curtly. "The world needs iron for its civilizations, and how is it going to get it if some of us don't go down into the earth and dig it out? Should we take turns doing it? Why don't we try that? I'll go down this week, and next week Andrew will take my place while I preach for him, and the next week Stuart can . . ."

"Yes, that would be a fine plan," said Rhena. "But next you'll be wanting me to go into the mines and serve my week. And I would be willing," she added with a deep sadness, which sometimes came upon her, "if I thought it would help to solve the problem, and make life better and a more blessed reality to thousands of souls than it is now. After all, how little we actually seem to be doing to answer the problem. Dear friends, we need more wisdom, and we've not yet gone to the eternal Source of all strength and truth as we should have. Before we discuss our plans any longer, don't you think we ought to pray?"

The request seemed so simple and natural that all immediately bowed their heads as they sat around the table. Rhena prayed first, but was followed by Andrew, then Eric, and finally Stuart. Each petition was straightforward and asked for wisdom and a better understanding of God's will. Interestingly enough, the somewhat foggy thinking they had been experiencing seemed to clear up after pausing to pray to their Father. During the rest of the afternoon, their hearts and minds seemed more open, and they continued asking for God's divine wisdom in using all their talents and property for the greater benefit of humanity.

About four o'clock, as Eric and Andrew were getting up to go, the doctor came by to check on Louise. He had come into the house without being noticed and had entered the library as Stuart was once again discussing plans for the hospital. He walked in just as Stuart said, "It will be great for the doctor. It will keep him busy, and he won't have to endure those terrible rides across the hills during the winter anymore."

"If you're talking about that plan of yours of turning this house into a hospital and shutting me up in it for the rest of my life, you're wasting your time and breath," said the doctor gruffly. "I simply won't do anything of the kind. I can't live without fresh air."

The doctor looked sternly at the little group around the table. It was raining hard outside and he was dripping wet. Before he removed his coat and went to see Louise, he stood there looking quite uncomfortable. The rain had run from the brim of his old hat onto his right ear, and any shirt collar he had before his arrival had long since melted away around his neck and was now underneath the folds of his overcoat.

"Doctor, you say the rest of us should use more sense. Look at you!" exclaimed Stuart. "Here you are soaked through and through. And knowing you, you won't have a dry thread on again until tomorrow, or even next week, for all I know. You'll catch your death of cold this way."

"Have you ever known me to catch a cold?"

"Anyway," Stuart continued, changing the subject, "this place we are arranging for you will be a comfortable haven for you the rest of your life. You're getting too old, Doctor, to expose yourself to another winter."

"I'm not a big enough fool yet to be cooped up in a hospital. Besides, who will look after the men outside if I stay here all the time?" the doctor asked stubbornly.

"We could find someone. There are plenty of young doctors who would love to begin a practice here," Stuart argued.

"Yes!" the doctor blurted out. "Young upstarts who have a lot of newfangled surgical instruments and are eager to try every one of 'em on every case they get, whether it's rheumatism or a liver problem. I was talking with one of 'em last winter, and he wanted me to swallow his latest contraption for operating on the throat with an electric light and battery combined, and I don't know what all! What'll become of my people if these fellows are turned loose on 'em with their inventions? No, sir! I don't intend to expose 'em to any such risks. The mines around here are dangerous enough, but a new doctor with a lot of brand-new instruments is too much even for Champion."

"But you're always grumbling about the hard work, and when we finally want to provide a comfortable place for you to practice, you won't take it," said Stuart, firing a parting shot as the doctor headed toward the hall.

"A comfortable place! Stuart, you know I'd rather die from tumbling with Ajax and all into an old shaft on my way to set Lew Trethven's leg the nineteenth time than get petrified to death in the best hospital on earth!" retorted the doctor.

Perhaps falling in a shaft was how he would die, but there was no persuading the doctor to abandon his outdoor work helping the miners. After all, it was out there that the doctor felt the love of humanity and its hunger for love, and nothing but that would ever satisfy him. The thought of turning over "the people of his parish," as he often called them, to strangers was a thought he could not endure. He had cared for them too long, and as long as God would allow, he wanted to continue tumbling through snowdrifts and wading through gorges to still claim the privilege of calling his "parishioners'" names and loving them.

So the short summer went by swiftly and Stuart's plans for the hall continued, although he seemed to encounter some new problem each day. It took a growing sense of purpose on his part, coupled with Rhena's great love for him, to keep him calm and hopeful. Using God's money for the good of the people who had the greatest needs was not an easy accomplishment. He had discussed a profit-sharing plan with Eric and some of the other miners. It was one of the many plans he was determined to try in the future. Yet he seemed hindered most in his efforts to exercise what he called his "stewardship" by the very men he was the most eager to help. Many of the miners would not consent to any improvement in their cabins and did not welcome Stuart's attempt to drain some of the nearby swamp. Another continual foe was the saloon, which never paused in its work of destruction, always attempting to tear down every good work.

But as fall came and the great building began to take shape, and other possibilities for the future of Champion came to him, Stuart settled one thing very clearly and firmly. Whatever his plans might be, and however much he might stumble or make mistakes in the days to come, he knew that he must give an account to God for the use of his money, brains, property, and anything else he possessed. After all, he owed it all to God, and in reality it all belonged to Him anyway. He was fully persuaded that his stewardship was a sacred thing and a very vital part of his Christian faith. Stuart had an overwhelming sense of peace once he rested on the conviction of dedicating all of his possessions to unselfish ends. He would use all God had given him for the good of humanity, as long as the Lord would give him the strength and wisdom to work out the details.

The special ways he spent God's money would often have to be an experiment and trial. Yet the exact way of using the money was not as important as his total willingness to use it as his brother's keeper. He often argued, and rightfully so, that if men of wealth would ever acknowledge that they were God's stewards, and were willing and eager to use their money and talents to the glory of God's kingdom here on earth, it would not be difficult to find the best way to use it. If someone desires to do God's will, he will soon find the proper way to do it. The greatest need is for that person to first be eager to do God's will.

The home he was building for Rhena and himself was built with the same idea that was now pervading his entire life. It was built as a home, but in such a way that its use would bless all of Champion. No one could have ever accused Stuart and Rhena of living in selfish or needless luxury. Every cent used in the building of their home was spent as if they were planning to receive the Lord Jesus Christ Himself as their most honored guest and offer Him a place of rest after a weary day spent in the world.

The day the Hall of Humanity was completed was a memorable day in the history of Champion. A miners' holiday was declared, and the building was crowded the entire day with the men and their families. Stuart, with the help of Andrew and Eric, had planned a dedication service to be held in the large auditorium that evening. He had left early, leaving Rhena with Louise, who had been more restless than usual that day. As the doctor had predicted, Louise had lingered through the summer, but her health continued to gradually fail. No one had taken better care of her than Rhena, and tonight was no exception. She stayed with her until she became quiet, and then left her in the care of a nurse before joining Stuart at the hall.

The miners had formed a marching band and had been preparing for some time to take part in the occasion, at Stuart's request.

They marched into the hall early and took their places on the platform. The Salvation Army also proudly arrived, marching down the main aisle to the familiar beat of their bass drum. They were led by their major, who still had some doubt about moving into their new quarters without first breaking some of the furniture simply to make it feel more like home. However, he had consented to try it as it was, but if everything seemed just too good, Stuart had arranged to lease the old Army Hall for them once again.

The doctor had been found attending to someone out in the hills, and Stuart had persuaded him to be on the platform, but was unable to prevail upon him to offer any remarks.

"I'm no speaker. Don't ask me, Stuart. If anyone in the audience is sick or feels bad after you, Eric, and Andrew have talked to 'em, I'll do my best for 'em. But it would be like performing an operation on their skulls without using anesthesia if I tried to talk to them. It would simply be too painful for all of us. I'll agree, however, to yell at any good points the rest of you make if I can see 'em without a microscope."

Andrew spoke briefly on the value of the building in providing opportunities for Christian service. He stressed the fact that it was not money that would make the plans for the building succeed, but real Christian men and women, who would pour their hearts into the work the hall was to represent.

Eric then delivered a very powerful speech. He finally seemed to be over his disappointment and bitterness, and he was nearly as popular as ever with the men. He shared his intention to continue working in the mines, which, of course, would help him to someday become an even stronger leader in the miners' eyes. At the end of his speech he took the opportunity to say some beautiful things about Stuart and his desire to help all the people in the community.

Stuart spoke last and felt this was one of the most important occasions of his life. He was profoundly moved as he stood to face the audience. He knew them as the same audience he had seen at the meetings in the square, at the railroad station, at the park, and in the union hall at DeMott. They were the same rough, solemn, and impassive crowd, yet with an occasional face that would light up when deeply moved by a human touch. It was the same, and yet it was different. To Stuart it spoke of opportunities, for he now saw humanity through new eyes.

He spoke well, simply and with strength. Rhena felt a whole new sense of admiration for her strong and handsome husband as he stood there before the people he loved. The depth and beauty of her love for him grew that night, and more than once tears came to her eyes as she listened, hearing him share very plainly his great desires for the betterment of mankind. The men also listened with nearly breathless anticipation, and when he finished, they began to applaud and cheer. The ovation was deafening, and Stuart, overwhelmed by the emotion of the night, finally sat down and covered his face with his hands.

It then seemed quite natural for Rhena to ask the audience to bow their heads for prayer. The people themselves felt nothing would have been more fitting as a closing for the occasion than for Rhena to kneel with the Salvation Army kneeling around her, just as they used to do. As they knelt, she prayed more earnestly than ever for abundant life to be given to them all. Even while Rhena was still on her knees, the audience, without fully knowing the reason for it, felt that the building was truly consecrated in a very solemn and profound sense to the humanity in whose honor it was named. Then Andrew, sensing that the time had come to close the service, proclaimed a beautiful benediction and blessing.

At that precise time, when Rhena was kneeling before that large, silent crowd of miners, the doors of Aunt Royal's mansion in New York were being thrown open to one of the first events of the society season. There the social butterflies of the world had gathered, with their diamonds and silk, their beautiful music and laughter, and vanity upon vanity. They were adorned with the impressive power that is always so apparent with the rich at leisure. They ate, drank, gossiped, and danced as if the world were all play, and the primary duty of every man and woman were to be as free from problems and sacrifice as possible. Aunt Royal was at her best, for her trip abroad had given her weary nerves a much needed rest. She was ready for another season of merriment, parties, and fun.

"By the way," asked a young man during the evening, who had also been abroad for several months, "where is that charming niece of yours, Louise, who used to visit you occasionally?"

Aunt Royal turned somewhat pale. "You haven't heard? She's an invalid and now lives with her brother in Champion. It's doubtful that she will survive the winter. The winters in Champion are horrible. I spent one there and it nearly killed me."

"We're certainly thankful it was only one winter! How could we have spared you here in New York?" was the polite reply.

Aunt Royal smiled at the compliment, while the guests with their elegance, and the party with its flowers, perfume, and carefree attitude from the world's woes, nearly shut out the picture in her mind. She could still vaguely see her young niece, who in genuine agony knelt by her in this very room not long ago, and begged for . . . *But—strike up the band,* she thought. *Play the music faster and faster. Let us eat, drink, and be merry, for tomorrow we die.*

The musicians at Aunt Royal's had begun the soft, dreamy waltzes just as Stuart and Rhena walked into the library of the Duncan house in Champion. The nurse had sent word for them to hurry home, for she had seen a serious change in Louise's condition as the evening wore on. They went immediately to her bedroom.

They did not need a doctor with a solemn look on his face to know that the end was near. Louise was propped up on her pillows, and her eyes still glowed with the fever of madness that had long been destroying her.

"Come!" she cried in a strange and irritating voice. "We'll be late. Don't you hear the clock ticking?" Everyone in the room suddenly jumped as the clock in the hall struck eleven at that very moment. "Come! Give me my gloves and fan, and tell Jem to drive around at once. Be careful of my dress! Do I look all right? The dance will be started. We will miss the first one. How slow you are! I wanted lilies of the valley, and you sent up the freesias. I don't think they are a bit pretty. Doctor, you said not to forget my coat when I went out to the carriage. It seems cold! What's the matter? Hey! I hear the music! Why don't they play faster? It's not fast enough."

She suddenly stopped talking and her eyes opened more widely. She seemed to see something the others did not. Then she cried in a terrible voice, "Aunt Royal! Hal! I'm going mad! I am mad! Doctor! Doctor! Save me!"

Then Louise fell back, and the doctor, who had arrived just in time to hear her ramblings, shuddered and for a moment buried his face in his hands. Stuart had never seen Dr. Saxon do that before, and when he raised his head, no one needed to ask him when the end would come—for it was already there. She had died, as the doctor had supposed she would, suddenly and painlessly. Her life had gone out like a flickering candle on a cold winter's night, when the front door of the mansion would be swiftly opened and then closed again on the icy, blowing wind.

"Tell the musicians to play a little faster," said Aunt Royal, just a few minutes later. And so they did.

When morning came—gray and cold—Stuart was standing by the window of the bedroom, exactly as he had done one year before when his father had died. Louise lay there, and now that her troubled life had ended, her face seemed nearly as beautiful as when

Stuart first saw her on his return from Europe. The jewels were still around her neck and the bracelets were on her wrists, while the freesias, which she had complained about, lay across her chest.

Stuart looked through the window and saw that a crowd of miners had come down the road and were silently standing in front of the mansion. He greatly appreciated their purpose in coming so early in the morning, knowing they were wanting to share his grief and to express their sympathy, even before going to their day's work.

"Tell the men to come up. I'll be glad to thank them for coming," he said to a servant.

At that moment Rhena walked in, and Stuart said to her, "God has truly given you to me, or else this would be more than I could bear." He stood with his arm around her as the tears of his humanity streamed down his face at the sight of the pale clay still lying on the bed. Then he turned toward the foyer with his wife.

"God is merciful," she said. "He has given us something to live for, and we will invest our lives in doing His will."

"Yes," replied Stuart, "humanity, after all, is worth saving and is worth living for. We are our brothers' keepers. There is nothing greater in all the world than the love of God for His children, and the love of His children for one another." And with those words he walked out and shut the door upon the dead and its past, and with the woman he loved by his side faced the living and its future.

notes

Chapter 1

1. This incident is based on fact. The writer of this story was a witness to a gathering of iron miners in the great strike of July 1895, where one of the miners offered this prayer, at Negaunee, Michigan, July 24, 1895.

Chapter 10

1. Meaning the church universal.

about
the
author

C harles M. Sheldon was a minister at the Central Congregational Church in Topeka, Kansas, from 1889 until his death in 1946. He wrote many inspirational novels, including the all-time best-seller *In His Steps,* which was also the inspiration for the recent widely popular WWJD (What Would Jesus Do?) line of books and gifts. Sheldon wrote *His Brother's Keeper* in 1895, a year before he wrote *In His Steps.*

about the editor

Jim Reimann is a past chairman of the Christian Booksellers Association and the former owner of one of the largest and most successful Christian bookstores in the country. He currently works as a writer and Christian retailing consultant. He is the editor of the updated editions of *My Utmost for His Highest* and *Streams in the Desert,* which together have more than 2.5 million copies in print.